The Constitution of Our Soul

The Constitution of Our Soul

Destiny's Deliverance of Our Soul's Rights

Kristy Kaye

BALBOA.
PRESS

A DIVISION OF HAY HOUSE

Balboa Press books may be ordered through booksellers or by contacting:

Balboa Press
A Division of Hay House
1663 Liberty Drive
Bloomington, IN 47403
www.balboapress.com
1-(877) 407-4847

ISBN: 978-1-4525-0286-1 (sc)
ISBN: 978-1-4525-0285-4 (e)

Because of the dynamic nature of the Internet, any web addresses or links contained in this book may have changed since publication and may no longer be valid. The views expressed in this work are solely those of the author and do not necessarily reflect the views of the publisher, and the publisher hereby disclaims any responsibility for them.

The author of this book does not dispense medical advice or prescribe the use of any technique as a form of treatment for physical, emotional, or medical problems without the advice of a physician, either directly or indirectly. The intent of the author is only to offer information of a general nature to help you in your quest for emotional and spiritual well-being. In the event you use any of the information in this book for yourself, which is your constitutional right, the author and the publisher assume no responsibility for your actions.

Any people depicted in stock imagery provided by Thinkstock are models, and such images are being used for illustrative purposes only.
Certain stock imagery © Thinkstock.

Printed in the United States of America

Balboa Press rev. date: 11/15/2011

Dedication

To each of those unknown heroes who remain anonymous and yet who perform their miracles for us with unconditional love, accompanying us on all our journeys in every moment of our lives and even beyond until they escort us home.

"My compatriots, I offer you the sound of your soul's music."

Anonymous

Contents

Our Thinking Nature

Technique #4: Sense, Organize,
Act—a Way to Uplift Your
Energy

The First Steps to Creating Change

Overview of importance of these two qualities

How and
why loyalty is
essential to the evolvement of the soul

Sincerity Overview

Awakening

Technique #5: Self-Loyalty—
Redeeming the Soul Focus

Sincerity

A Cautionary Note

Technique #6: "Healing the Past"

Karma

Pride

Discernment

Technique #7: Clearing
Technique

Grief

Our Two Natures in Review

The Constitution of Our Soul

A Journal.

Preface

The Constitution of Our Soul: is the untold, in-depth truth of the journey of the soul's awakening to the reality of living in two worlds at once: a physical world—planet Earth—and a spiritual world—the universe—and the conflict these dual existences can create.

The book patiently and persistently winds its way through these unchartered waters, dispelling myths and mysteries on its path. Most of these ideas of life, summarily dismissed as fantasies, have probably been the mainstay of our belief systems for centuries. Despite the awkwardness of this, we may find that in reclaiming our lost truth, a pervading feeling of relief is perceived as possibilities of a new and invigorated lifestyle, evolving into the super beings who we really are, unfold. These alternatives can only open in the demise of myths, thus helping to produce a paradigm shift that aligns us with our inner truth, the *Constitution of Our Soul.*

By investing in the truth of our spiritual journey rather than accepting blindly the belief systems of others, we learn how to initiate freedom for ourselves, losing unwelcome harassments we may have previously believed impossible to shift. We can then breathe a sigh of relief as we discover conceivable options for living our potential and what it takes to do that.

In this world of illusionary ideals, we may have believed or lived worries, uncertainties, anxieties, or dread of the unfamiliar because the simple truth of the power of who we are may have been buried in all manner of dogma. This book opens a potential opportunity for us to unlock the door to all the mysteries that have captivated us into a maze-like state, living repetitive days "Groundhog Days" of our lives. These pursuits diminish the essence of our energy as we attempt to maintain the costly energy discharge in living illusion.

We can further discover the only true pathway to freedom is forged by delving within, through the often-neglected and enigmatic pathways of our soul. Our own constitutions, the book reveals, are conversant with the wisdom necessary to empower us to open up this vault of secrets, unleashing our inner force as we do so. Participation in the treasury we have within can guide us to return to the euphoric space, our inherent right, once we reclaim our lost spiritual real estate. Each of these subjects is covered in depth within this book. Also included are life-changing techniques to facilitate the process of unfolding the wisdom of our constitutions. The reason these techniques can invigorate our lives is because they are guided and instigated by the miraculous and transformational energy of the "Spirit" (Holy Spirit). Each of us has this endowment available once we decide to invest in ourselves and live our constitution with sincerity.

The book shows us how we all must pass through the Gates of Awakening on our journey back to enlightenment. As we commence our journey as a baby when we incarnate onto planet Earth and awaken to a strange environment, we absorb a step-by-step instruction; similarly, our soul designs its journey back to its magnificence with juvenile steps, each of them specific, necessary, special, and profound.

For those curious about the term "awakening," this is the soul's true birth or burst of consciousness, the first step in the system of evolvement each soul moves through each lifetime. It is when our third eye begins to open and function with insights. There is a system of ascending steps for this as we gradually become more aware of a different dimension than the intellectual one we have predominantly been living in.

We may see, feel, hear, or know of confused souls, suspended around us, of whom we may be apprehensive. Once we understand who they are, we can grasp the realities of why they are there and learn to invoke the spiritual support we have to buffer our energy from their engagement. Techniques for this are provided in the book in addition to explanations of concepts (misunderstandings) that can anchor these souls to us.

The book demonstrates how we have become desensitized through ideologies on our journeys (lifetimes) through planet Earth and how such misadventures have helped fashion the maze we are presently living.

It touches on how we can assimilate mass consciousness behaviour as if it were our own individual plan. We can use such examples as following the same news and TV shows, wearing the same brand of shoes, listening to the same music, thinking the same thoughts, watching the same movies, and reading the same books concurrently with many other millions of people around the world, as well as consciously dismantling our integrity with our constitutions in seeking to "fit in."

Because of this, we may have less of a propensity to do some individual soul-searching or to trust our inner truth, which may feel drowned out by this stereotypic life, although ninety per cent of who we are is totally out of alignment with living these delusions.

The book involves itself in how each of us is unique and individual with a special message to share with our fellow man. It is this innate desire to manifest the individuality of the wisdom of our constitutions, which bubbles within that can influence us to strive to be appreciated or become famous in the absence of acknowledgment for our prudence.

The book demonstrates for us factually that, until we understand what it is, we may not have any real success in our life endeavours, make names for ourselves or find the elusive fulfilment which only our own soul-discovery will provide the impetus for us to live.

> Wood burns because it has the proper stuff in it; and a man becomes famous because he has the proper stuff in him.
>
> —Johann Wolfgang von Goethe

We are possibly unaware of the energy we call Spirit (or Holy Spirit) a general term for an enlightened energy which surrounds us and everybody else; it feeds our souls and is forever evolving our environments with or without our participation. If we progress and allow ourselves to be challenged by it in our daily lives, we will feel our inherent joy, fulfilment, and contentment. The specific energy that our angels use to guide us is adequately explained in the book.

If we are unaware or unwilling to change with the spirit which unfolds and refines us, the greater the disparity between our equilibrium and the level of refinement of the energy feeding our souls can become. Therefore, our sense of anxiety can become more intense as we source this disconnectedness deliberately. Eventually through adversity, this pressure can make us more sincere to seek answers to the questions spiritual awakening engenders, but our pathways in choosing this course take us via the back roads to enlightenment.

As we evolve, our angels ensure that our participation is at a level we are ready for by guiding us through our life's learning lessons. In the beginning, they offer us small steps, and as we develop more illumination, we are able to expand our awareness of a greater consciousness of planetary energy; freedom is its consequence.

> Difficulties strengthen the mind, as labour does the body.
>
> —Seneca

The mechanics of awakening are covered in depth in the book because it is where all our spiritual conversations begin.

Introduction to Awakening

Wisdom is not a product of schooling but of the lifelong attempt to acquire it.

—Albert Einstein

Anyone may, equally as I have done, study in the University of Spirit; it is the birthright of each of us. We may need guidance to find the pathways there because they are often fraught with our own confusion about who we are, where we came from, and where we are going. This book can help us remember again the unique system of Spirit. Just as our bodies have a modus operandi involving a profound physical system, our souls are a replica of the universal system of Spirit. Our body is the servant of our soul and mirrors our state of consciousness. We can refer to this as the level of our awareness of the truth of ourselves and our existence. Even the depth of each breath we inhale is inhibited or expanded by our awareness of our soul, as are all physical, emotional, and spiritual encounters in our lives.

Without recognition of these systems and its eventual self realisation, we can encounter deceit, mistrust, and frustration. We can't learn enlightenment through reading this or any other book, but rather we can develop a predisposition for it, thus allowing the process of awakening to unfold its petals like the lotus flower, permitting the intelligent energy that feeds our soul to present its scrolls as the timing for them arises.

Our angels author much of the script provided for our beginning steps. As we progress on our pathways beyond the scope of this book, our inherent limitless natures can resurrect their abilities to write our own screenplays for our lives and their opportunities to heal and reveal. We can then, in time, with refinement and dedication, even recognise our potential to stand shoulder to shoulder with our angels.

Because the pathway to enlightenment begs our commitment, there are tools and techniques provided to make each step a solid foundation to enable its ensuing progression. We cannot take shortcuts either because our ability to memorize or recite knowledge of soul-discovery is useless to us without "experiencing," which is when our energy physically moves to embrace a new truth. For example, we can recall when we have momentous changes or challenges in our lives that force a dynamic shift in nurturing (we lose or gain a loved one), have careers or family life adjustments (such as parent upheavals for a child). These changes orchestrated by outside influences or at least not usually incidental to our conscious decision-making, but rather delivered by destiny, may either be heralded as tragedies or blessings.

I feel confident each of us has had his or her share of experiencing, which has probably been through unwelcome learning lessons. Even though these life-encounters stimulated consternation at the time, they possibly delivered us to a slightly higher state of consciousness.

The book demonstrates an easier way to grow spiritually if we are in coordination with our team of angels and can then choose the manner in which we wish to learn our lessons to initiate the necessary changes in our lives. We can, with spiritual evolution, learn to control our fates.

This book helps us to establish an attentiveness to the multiple messages we receive from our intellect and its doctrines versus spontaneous impressions from our feelings and guided insights from our angels. These inspirations reveal our soul's constitution and contribute extensively to the core of self and soul-discovery. The disparity between our two natures is covered in depth in this book.

What shall it profit a man if he gains the whole world but loses his soul?

—Jesus Christ

We can call the energy that supports our revelations our inner guidance, angels, or some of us may be more comfortable with God, but whatever we call it, we all somehow yearn for more of these occurrences or miracles. This book will with our commitment, I believe, assist in opening the natural pathway of encountering this phenomenon, which magnifies with our discoveries.

He who knoweth his own self, knoweth God.

—Prophet Muhammad

The Constitution of Our Soul has been written in layman's terms as an introduction to the progression of awakening and explains its steps. By using the user-friendly techniques presented as part of the book, one may find the progression of awakening more easily able to accelerate one's own spiritual journey, which is the aim of the book.

The nature of information made available is delivered in a detached way, ensuring the writer and the readers are conversing but are not interconnected in a dependency. I want your journey to be what it needs to be for you—an empowering and limitless adventure. You truly deserve it.

Primarily the process begins with healing yourself. We call this the inflow levels of consciousness. This is a broad term to explain the process of healing otherwise known as the steps to maturity or lower levels of consciousness.

The book is layered in its presentation of the steps to awakening where it begins its journey at the 'me' level of understanding. It progresses to share deeper insights on the same subjects as this information is absorbed. This is how our feelings operate enabling comprehension and avoiding overwhelm. The stairway to enlightened understanding is then designed to fit our unique stride and pace.

For those who have found real strength in religion, our growth spiritually is never about one ideal, religion, or cause being better than another. Each of them has truth but not all the truth. A person may in those circumstances hunger for more information without necessarily wanting to change his or her style of worship. Whatever we do is okay as long as we acclaim it so. It is always our choice the pathways we undertake.

The book merely focuses on our relationship with ourselves and how essential it is for any spiritual advancement. As we flourish in our understanding that we are a reflection of God, it is easier to trust our inner truth. This book may prompt us to regularly clean the mirror of this reflection metaphorically speaking to enhance this realization. We need to wipe off the marks on our mirror that may have obscured our belief in our integrity and ourselves. We need to forgive the past, whatever it is, and move on. It sounds simple, because it is if we allow it to be.

The Constitution of Our Soul is not a personal journal but rather a journal of facts recorded, and with inspiration from the reader, it will open the door to a search for greater consciousness and the amazing, miraculous changes it can foster.

These facts have been gathered from the experiences of the writer and many sincere people using advanced tools and techniques who openly shared their steps in an organized spiritual system of self-development. The information in the book embodies their observations of the ultimate freedom they witnessed from each investment of their own inner truth, even sometimes from small encounters of soul-discovery like learning a technique, sharing in a course, or participating in group work.

The writer has earned the privilege to channel the Holy Spirit; (I call Spirit), which is writing down their words. The book demonstrates the various levels of self-understanding and healing one may choose to undertake to enable the steps to perspicacity. There is no ceiling to our growth spiritually. Each person can attain whatever he or she sincerely desires in evolvement. Each step encompasses larger collaborations with our own veracity.

Indeed, the number of people who it has been my privilege to observe become a channel for their angels in certain circumstances is too numerous to recount in detail. It is the usual advancement of soul-discovery. It is obviously another amazing attribute of our natural inheritance of intelligence.

The information in the book although from the source of Spirit in parables and symbols is interpreted into an understandable language. This process encompassed steps beginning at the training in self and soul-discovery through a personal healing process and then developing, often through pain and persistence, self-understanding at more evolved and enlightened states. Having shared with others at all diversified stages of growth, has facilitated its consolidation at high levels of consciousness thus enabling me to write this journal detailing the steps to enlightenment.

Each of us are involved in the process of stretching our aura back into shape and regaining its point instead of living with a round and generally undirected soul shape. There are no exceptions to this spiritual law, and although it may not present initially as a feel-good happening, its ultimate changes are miraculous.

In humility, we who have found the pathway to illumination, whether by turmoil, unavoidable life-scrapes of pain and hardship, the good fortune to have been guided by a mentor, or all three, as in my case and attaining an enviable constant angelic presence, now endeavour to assist others to make the journey and put some footprints in the sand for them to follow. Acquiring freedom through ascending higher levels of consciousness narrows the option of pathways to travel in life deliberately delivering us to the task of ensuring we encompass educating others on the steps to freedom as our priority. The universe becomes more present than our life on planet Earth, and we naturally are driven to liberate others. As I and many before me have found, those of you who find the pathways to a greater consciousness will similarly feel compelled in time to share your insights.

Every man is a channel through which heaven floweth.
—Ralph Waldo Emerson

The words of the book have found their own journey onto the pages. My commitment has been to turn up to facilitate their manifestation. From my early life, I was always aware of an unseen person guiding me. As a young child, I truly believed it was God, because such was my teaching. Now I know it was my angels delivering me to my soul's constitution. My angels gave their dedication and total commitment to assist my individual quest for the truth obviously knowing I would one day share it with others. To do this I needed each of these angels for the wisdom of their personal experience.

For the whole of my life, I have been inspired, motivated, and renewed through learning about people. My father was a people person, and he always received people searching for answers with enthusiasm, driven by a generous and caring nature and an open-hearted, giving Christian way. He was fascinated by the revelations I shared. I openly channelled whatever I heard without any reservation. I knew two priests, endearing friends of my parents, who were intrigued by my spontaneous sharing. They spent each available lunch hour with me at the school I attended, and I subsequently returned home on these days with my lunch uneaten. One remained a good friend into my teens until I moved away from my hometown. At an early age and in the right environment, an intellect is not any form of restriction. I lived in a pure world. There were no evil people—at least that is what I believed, and fortunately, my location was very safe.

With my siblings, I explored well beyond the boundaries of our home as the years went on. I invested in friendships with all manner of people during these formative years.

I began school at a very early age because the school's committee felt my mother was under pressure with managing her children and wanted to show their support for my father, who was extremely active in the community and in particular for the school I attended. As I became a teenager, I wanted to be a missionary. My parents would not agree. My father was not going to allow me to go to some strange country where my life might be threatened, and he was adamant about this. I was too young to legally make my own decisions. I therefore abided by his.

When I was eighteen I followed the direction of my angels courageously and moved away from the security of my small town environment to a city. Here I became ambitious and slowly disengaged from my connectedness with the world of Spirit to pursue a career path. I became skilled at certain aspects of the law and chose to work for people who I could learn from and only for as long as the education lasted. One person I worked with was a defence lawyer, and at his office, I met the criminals who were on the front page of the news the next day. This provided endless fascination for me as I read countless depositions and gave my opinion on cases. Inexperienced as it was, I had an uncanny insight into legal matters. (My mentor later told me I had spent many lifetimes as a lawyer and he engaged this sagacity in some of his personal legal matters.)

There were all manner of interesting people in my life now. I associated with lawyers, musicians (some famous ones), politicians and actors. I was learning about people and their lives and I was experiencing the darkness, a very necessary step in my spiritual advancement. It came as a shock initially to discover people deceived calculatedly and with deliberate intent to gain unfairly. I learnt many of the vices my small town childhood overlooked—

manipulation, greed, various types of concern, anxiety, insecurity, and many other emotional concepts. People were drawn to me for answers and I readily supplied them. I was yet to discover my own personal maze and concepts of misunderstanding.

I was absorbed in learning about life and people. I wanted to fit in. When I married, I entered the world of business and began to embrace the confused planetary values of acquiring wealth for security having lost the confidence of my connectedness. I became preoccupied with building businesses almost initially as a hobby although it soon became my new passion. This helped educate me about people and their tendencies in these involvements, and with experience my business training became more comprehensive. I moved further and further away from my connectedness and entered a grey period where I was beginning to fit in as a model citizen living the illusions like everyone else around me.

I moved to Europe and started a business there for a few years. I learned their laws and ways and a new language, with the assistance of my husband, adding more depth to my business management experience. When I returned home, I successfully began businesses that offered more financial security. I travelled, holidayed abroad, had children, and built a life around educating them and living the good life for some years as I believed it to be at the time. I was on this course when my mentor found me. He came deliberately and never shared his true identity initially, but from our first meeting touching his energy and the resultant memories of who I was and what I needed to do this lifetime came flooding back into my life again and my attitude toward it changed forever. An unseen force was again guiding me out of the grey world of conformity I had descended into.

It was two years after this first surreptitious meeting before I began to search in earnest for my mentor yearning to live the purpose I had abandoned. I was finally awake spiritually and ready to rediscover my mission. It was easy to locate him, even though he resided in another country I had never been to. He had illuminated the pathways for me to follow despite me believing at the time I was using my own initiative. After four days in his instruction, the course of my whole life altered dramatically because my attitude to myself had made a paradigm shift.

Thus began my true journey of soul-discovery. With my mentor's guidance, I learnt about myself, my past lives, my tendencies, and my sins against my inner truth and myself and began to dismantle the web of misinformation I was living in. At times I thought it was hell, and other times, when the clouds parted, it was heaven. For the difficult times, I had an insatiable thirst for the policies of my soul's constitution, which rode over any obstacles as they presented themselves. It was easy for me to uncover the pages of the past with the backing of my angels and with the tools my mentor's courses had provided.

After an intensive eight years of training me as a metaphysician, my mentor passed on, and my life entered a new phase of education. It still involved input from him now in a different dimension and my angels but was more specific. It was not limited to what I desired for my own self-healing but was now to be of benefit to the planetary consciousness. I was following in the footsteps of my mentor writing courses for the spiritual advancement of others. He did not want me to pursue promotion of the courses that educated me. They were the 'old' energy he told me, no longer relevant. We were on new pathways with the new millennium. My preparation to live this chapter of my purpose was complete they informed me. I personally did not believe so. My years of avoidance and hiding in the huge shadow he cast ended in that moment. All pathways to escape my fate were eliminated, and only those that culminated in a forward movement to my purpose remained illuminated. I took the instruction of these new dynamic spiritual courses for myself first verifying their potency through self-administration and then I shared it with others close by. Those who were similarly trained as I was were overwhelmed by their potency and joined me on my journey to share them.

During this time, my businesses faltered through neglect but I couldn't change my fate because all the passageways out of it were blocked by energy. Whatever I did to resurrect their continuance in one day was reversed by my angels the next. If one ever doubted the power of Spirit, the details of my story at this time would permit them to truly question their scepticism. My angels wanted me to live my purpose and this, my preoccupation with running my business, was interfering with it. What my intellect wanted became irrelevant and subservient to my purpose.

My mentor helped to coach me out of my small-picture complacency and apprehension. I found my old passion to help people spiritually ignited again. I was channelling information that opened an insightful awareness of how to heal influences that distorted one's belief in oneself. I actually had new, dynamic tools to help people to accelerate the process to reclaim their inner beauty. This was a powerful and potent armoury to possess to fight and combat planetary illusion and certainly richer in content than what I myself had access to whilst growing spiritually until this time. It was the discovery of a lifetime.

> Beauty is not in the face. Beauty is a light in the heart.
> —Kahlil Gibran

What do I do with it?

I could keep it for myself, to help me refine, and for those whose search brought them to my door, or I could make it available for many others. But this latter idea involved risks. Was I willing to take them? No, I was not. I tried to inspire others already involved in helping people spiritually to do it for me, but my mentor's organisations fell into bickering and division without his leadership. No one could fill his shoes. And when it was delivered to the justice department to rule on ownership of his materials, I knew that this passageway was closed to this new and essential energy. The big picture Spirit who shape planetary education and my angels were not going to walk me through that door of the past where there was dissension, accusations of theft, and court cases. Only through the process of force did I slowly find my own new path to sharing these courses.

I had dozens of excuses and justifications for my inaction. As I took each courageous step, my angels guiding me respectfully, I felt exhilarated. I cursed my trepidation and lack of trust and acknowledged what I was missing out on. As with all my discoveries in life thus far, the decisions had already been made long before this body I was using had come to be. My rebellion constituted a costly waste of time. Throughout my lifetime, I recognized my tendency to procrastinate with my purpose. Unfortunately, at this moment, its grip on me was extensive.

I began educating people, and it seemed to me to be masses of people, more thousands than tens of thousands but surely enough for a lifetime I believed. But after at least a decade or more of pursuing this with total accomplishment and fulfillment and refining my tools as I went, I was confident in sharing almost anything, but a new problem had manifested. It now ceased to fulfil me. I was almost bored. It could no longer allow my life to feel challenged or give me butterflies or to feel the excitement and anticipation rising within with each new step.

Realizing this, I began to question what was next. Why were my angels changing the energy? Forcing my fate once again. They had worked tirelessly to deliver me to my purpose, and now the road was meeting a dead end. I had to ponder this, but I knew without asking my new opportunity was going to be some form of writing. I always knew this is what I would do; I saw visions of it in my youth. Up until now I had written courses and trained people to instruct these courses. The books I wrote which came into being through the pressure of searchers I never bothered to publish because I innately knew the timing and content weren't right. The time was coming, but it was somewhere in that safe and unresolved future.

Then the new messages I was receiving to write a particular book became more intense and deliberate, but I was paying lip service to these, not really advancing in the project. I was comfortable even if I wasn't challenged. Publishing a book seemed too much of a stretch of these comfort zones I relished.

One of my clients came to me for her next step spiritually and repeated the exact words my angels were telling me about the book I was to publish. I was covered in chills and goose bumps, and my aura felt like it was on fire all at once. Part of her planetary profession included promoting large events; she did come with experience. She was told to deliver this message to me. It was a surreal awareness, unsettling and disturbing. My private little inner rebellion was suddenly public and exposed. What else were my angels going to do to deliver me? I felt apprehensive again but excited, and the butterflies were back.

She kept respectfully asking me if I understood what her angels were telling her. She felt very responsible personally for the safe delivery of this important communication. I understood perfectly, and in that moment I knew this: the book and my fate were signed, sealed, and delivered. The other information I had already received from my angels was concerning the manuscript's completion, which was to be within a three-month period. Now I was going to have the real consequences of my procrastination. There was some necessary spiritual deadline the material was needed for. This was out of my realm of discernment at this moment, but from the past through experience, I had truly gained respect for these deadlines and their importance. I didn't need to know why.

Without hesitation, I began, and as I did so, the words materialized on the pages almost unaided, as if they had been suspended in time and space waiting for me to pen them.

I had to be reminded to write myself into this, the introduction, which was written as the book was finalized. It seems very irrelevant to me that this information about who I am and how I came to know what I know needs to be included.

My credentials from previous incarnations are impeccable, which I will not divulge now, as it is unnecessary and inappropriate. I had the same struggle as everyone else this lifetime to discover my path. I had no gifted passage, although a very difficult and lonely journey no doubt assisting me to harness resolve. I know now I was looking for my spiritual family in my early life, but they were not around me—only my father, one sibling, the priest, and two others. This has made me more humble and enthusiastic to follow the course of my purpose. There is nothing like the pain of breaking through the shell of one's ignorance spiritually to sow the seeds of sincerity. My heart bleeds when I hear of the personal struggles people have with themselves and the hardships life presents them with, it is my sincere wish that this book will assist them.

Despite my own difficulties, I was content up till now to allow the burden of making larger footprints in the process of educating others to fall to those more willing instead of owning what was delegated to me to share and participating in putting my small piece of the large mosaic of life in place, thus ensuring that others affected by this are successful in placing their part before it, around it, or after it.

And why, then, do we require knowing more of my story beyond these facts as part of the book's philosophy and aims? We don't. It is very ordinary anyway, up until my spiritual training. It is not about me. My involvements beyond being able to share the insights are immaterial to the outcome.

The book is about you and is for you, the reader. They are words not from me but from destiny itself, which each of us is empowered with designing. Through my experiences of them I have been able to highlight and explain their message. It is a journal to help you open to the story of you and offering potentialities of discovering your individual mysteries, opening the pages from your untold millenniums and lifetimes. Where were you? What were you doing? The answers to these questions can now become a real probability for you to discover. (We don't want to cloud this, your moment of truth, with debates about me and my individual journey or to render any distraction potency other than what you need for your own personal edification.)

Tools and techniques are presented to help you find out this innate knowledge. Every secret you desire to uncover you can find the answers for within you using your power and your deliberation, with you in control. How liberating is this piece of information? Even the facts of your childhoods, this one and others before it you have forgotten, are all stored in your soul part that travels with you from body to body and lifetime to lifetime. The smallest details can be illuminated as you open to your inner truth. Why would you not desire this truth? It is pivotal information to live inner peace in every moment of your life. Each person I meet, when he or she can touch his or her soul constitution and begin to become it, shows me profound insight into their wisdom. It is the way of it.

It astounds me that people with the necessary tools, and you don't use many, inhibit their investigation of themselves, instead returning to me for help because of a stumbling block they have encountered. It is usually a past life they are refusing to review, and all the joy and pain stored there is knocking on their door to be released. The book is as much for them, to remind them of what they know and the training they have, as it is to help those who truly desire to learn about who they are. Many of those trained as well as the newly awakened have waited a long time for this book. There were people from the past who were trained to be of service to others spiritually but unfortunately will go to their grave this lifetime holding the secrets of their training because of their inability to overcome their ego. To fill the void, I hope to inspire new people to train to fill their shoes for this, the most admirable and refined avocation of all, helping others grow spiritually. The rewards are not in earthly remuneration but pay huge dividends eternally.

We are all angels who have lost our way, and the sooner we find it, the easier our lives will become and the more affluent the energy feeding our souls will refine itself to. No wonder we have trouble in compromising these big energies we are by squashing them in the little square box our life has become. This is a spiritual fact that we are angels, not some illusory idea that was summarily invented and its relevancy is clarified throughout this book. It is a large responsibility to grasp when we accept this realization and no greater a burden for you than anyone before you. Although we can say if it is a new idea, you may find it an entertaining thought to engage daily in flying around this planet and the universe as you rediscover your wings. You will be able to appreciate this as a metaphor as you gather momentum by losing the weight of concepts that inhibit your freedom of flight.

Because we are in a new age of enlightenment with a new type of energy, the change of millennium now broadcasts, dissimilar to when I began my search, we have an innate desire to manage our own spiritual education. We are less likely to search for a guru or mentor to guide us. Rather, it is like negotiating a buffet style meal where we can select what we feel we want to ingest as we desire it. We don't have a use for any new religions to meet the new energy's criteria for spiritual growth.

We can see this reflected in the political spectrum, as across the globe everyone wants self-determination. We can witness the decline of organized religions if they are unable to define themselves for the new millennium and the inimitable success of those that can.

In this new energy thrust we feel personally elevated in comparison to the last millennium. It is faster in speed. This new millennium energy is very distinctive and compelling with an entirely different approach than the last millennium, but living it with misconception can render more difficulties and demands than before.

It is crucial the reader is always in the driver's seat, choosing the pathways of discovery he or she wishes to take. Our inner truth is a great driving force to carry us on our own unique life adventure.

Respecting that each of us has our own resource of wisdom, although we may not at this moment be in contact with it, does not mean we are any less a mortal than those who can. My own journey has reflected this.

The Constitution of Our Soul was written as an opportunity to present the truth for all readers to investigate pathways back home to their soul constitution, the purity of them. All of us are amazing souls with unlimited potential (an angel with a message of enlightenment). It is necessary for us to redeem our inner truth, which will help us revitalize our energy and stretch our aura back into shape as we recognize it. Each day offers a possibility of doing this in a new cultivated way, building upon our yesterdays.

> If the mind is to emerge unscathed from this relentless struggle with the unforeseen, two qualities are indispensible: first, an intellect that even in the darkest hour, retains some glimmerings of the inner light which leads to the truth; and second, the courage to follow this light wherever it may lead.
>
> —Carl von Clausewitz

Overview

The first chapter targets dismay at the process of transition, which we call death when we do not realize we are immortal and which we can manifest when we have little understanding about who we are, where we are going, and why we are here.

It is imperative we explain this reality of our existence because there can be many historic facts about ourselves we disconnect from because of apprehension. Once we have these realities and the what, when, where, and why of all we want to know, we can relax into a state of being confident of where we are going and why. Anytime we feel foreboding, it is because the facts of the situation are not clear. Usually they are shrouded by illusion.

> Death the last sleep? No, it is the final awakening.
> —Sir Walter Scott

To those who only made the journey this far: may your feet be light and swift on their steps to a greater consciousness.

Chapter One: The Seeds Of Our Search

*Every truth passes through three stages before it is recognized
in the first it is ridiculed, in the second it is opposed, in the
third it is regarded as self evident.*

—Arthur Schopenhauer

Have you ever wondered about life? I mean have you ever seen anyone have a perfect one? Is your life perfect? If not, you may have the same enquiries as many others, particularly when you awaken spiritually and begin to question the world around you.

Or if you feel your life is perfect at times, then perhaps it might be helpful to consider these questions:

o   Where do you come from?
o   Where are you going?
o   Why are you here on planet Earth?
o   Does your life have ups and downs? If so, why?
o   Who is pulling the strings (making your fate, so to speak)?
o   Why do things happen to you?

1

- o   Why don't things happen for you?
- o   Where does luck come from?
- o   Where does fate come from?
- o   Why do we even have a lifetime? What is having one all about?
- o   Why do we get old?
- o   Why do we get sick?
- o   Why do we die?
- o   Why do most people want to get married?
- o   Why don't some people get married?
- o   Why are we all different?
- o   Is there really a God? If there is, what is he doing all day?
- o   Why isn't he fixing things?
- o   Why do you want to know about your soul identity? How can it possibly help you?

The answer to each of these questions is all relative to you learning about you. It sounds crazy right?

Q: Why on earth would knowing about myself make a difference to finding answers to these questions? You might ask, "What possible influence could my identity have on any answer?"

> Nobody, as long as he moves about among the chaotic currents of life, is without trouble.
>
> —Carl Jung

A: Let's begin there. We can say who you are determines all your life encounters and even influences the questions you ask. Logically, then, we commence our journey into your world through the gateway to understanding whatever holds mysteries for you. This will already attempt to answer a multitude of questions. We are, of course, not referring to who you think you are but rather to who you really are—your hidden identity, which is perhaps the best kept secret of too many millenniums.

In this discovery lies most of your answers! You are a reflection of your environment, and it is a mirror image of you. Awareness of yourself automatically allows you to understand your world.

If it sounds like a mystery, there is a good reason for it, which this journal will attempt to uncover. You may require patience while we reacquaint you with your true discourse, the language of your feelings.

> The more unintelligent a man is, the less mysterious existence seems to him.
>
> —Arthur Schopenhauer

If you doubt the validity of this mission, believing you already hold the answers of relevance to your hidden identity, and question how this journal can help you authenticate anything consequential about yourself, we can acquaint you with the journey uncovered by others before you. Their discoveries opened the building blocks to enlightenment, including:

o   Learning how to open the genius within
o   How to live the fulfilment of being the real you instead of a diluted version
o   How to have success in all areas of your life through daily revelations
o   How to find real happiness in each moment of your life by unfolding your multiplicity
o   How to have meaningful relationships
o   How to love yourself and others

Do these sound like qualities of life you might be interested in? We are not talking motivational lingo here. You are not a puppet that can be pulled by strings. We are immersing ourselves in the adventurous exploration into the depths of you—into your soul and beyond.

If yes, to truly acquire them, these magical, elusive mysteries of self, or in other words to open to your potential, will depend on what you do now and in every other moment in your life from now on as you seek to understand yourself better. The real question that requires an affirmative is if you are willing to inject time and passion into unfolding you.

Is there anyone else it would benefit you more to invest in than yourself? If you are truly honest, you will have leapt to the awareness it is always only about you. You can't really appreciate others if you have not made the necessary discoveries of yourself. Equally, you can't receive love, despite how much you believe you are surrendering, if you don't love yourself. It is a hollow gesture. It's one of those universal laws we can't bend.

What really does illusion do for you? Does it tuck you into your bed at night, embrace your concerns, and comfort you to explain them away, hold your hand up the long climbs, ensuring it will catch you as you stumble, or wipe away your tears at your disappointments? No, your angels do this, and illusion rips into you when you are down, sits on you when you stumble, laughs at your disappointments, and pulls the ground from under you when you regain your balance. Then where do you wish to imbue your energy—into your inner truth and into the arms of your angels or in illusion where confusion enthusiastically anticipates your every misfortune?

> Mistakes are after all the foundations of truth, and if a man does not know what a thing is, it is at least an increase in knowledge if he knows what it is not.
>
> —Carl Jung

Being honest about your misunderstandings instead of living cover-ups is a large step to healing your life. Although your life may already feel tinged or filled with negativity and you may believe being positive is being enlightened, as we begin to evaluate, you may find this healing is really only skin deep. It is a great beginning and where we all start the large trek up the mountain to reach enlightenment. To truly make changes, it is necessary for us to dig into real honesty about our life and our concepts of misunderstandings and the deeds of antipathy we undertake that do not make us feel good or feel fulfilled and the ensuing cover-ups we invent that dilute the powerful being we are.

> Men occasionally stumble over the truth, but most of them pick themselves up and hurry off as if nothing happened.
>
> —Sir Winston Churchill

Your misdeeds are not you. Each of those you deliberately or indiscriminately inhibit the memory of has a multidimensional and universal explanation, the discovery of which, with a focus on living your destiny, can ultimately help calibrate your energy into who you really are, "a supreme being." This book was written primarily to stimulate your desire to unfold the truth of this energy identity and to open to the realization that within your energy purity, you are perfection; you have nothing averse to reconcile. As you read on, you may find you have unwittingly submitted yourself to outside management because you have not believed in this purity.

What you may choose to do as you clarify your inner truth and its sophisticated constitution is to identify any misunderstandings you may believe about your life, your habits, your character, your integrity, your confidence, depression, judgment, or imperfection and their influences that may be residing within you. Imagine if you do decide to invest in the real you; the steps on this pathway can enable you to regain your flawlessness. To maintain it, you may need to learn to give direction by using your inner authority to any situation or person who doesn't want to support this. You need to change your attitude to yourself and in doing this, facilitate and support any necessary changes in attitude toward you.

There are risks, the nature of which in time and with commitment, your aura can become like a potent weapon changing environments wherever you go to positive and powerful. Others may feel confronted by this. People find you a magnet and want to be around you. You have to share your insights to maintain the potency. You may have to buy more refined appliances, because your aura can continually break them. Public places you visit can fill up with people quickly after you enter, and you may then have difficulty being served. Wherever you go, property increases in value, and if you rent, this can be detrimental, as your rent increases.

It is a process of redeeming what you have pawned, one step at a time, of course. There are undoubtedly copious amounts of spiritual real estate you didn't know you owned before you to reclaim. It really is as simple as realizing how energy works, but it is a process to become skilled at living it and on occasions:

o   It may require of you to navigate a maze.
o   You may need to overcome an obstacle or blockage.
o   It may be an addiction to negativity to give up.
o   It may be a truth to recognize, which may have become all dressed up in a fantasy.

> Be a Columbus to whole new continents and worlds within you, opening new channels not of trade, but of thought. Every man is the lord of a realm beside which the earth empire of the Czar is but a petty state, a hummock left by the ice.
>
> —Henry David Thoreau

Let us look at the alternative to soul-discovery, which may involve being complacent with our lives today. We can presume who we think we are today is enough for us to subsist on. We are not inquisitive beyond our present consciousness, and then let us pretend further we are content with this status quo. What happens now? That's it then? What you see is all you encompass; there is nothing more to it? How does it make you feel? Fulfilled? Empty? Disappointed? Relieved?

To truly test if it is your truth, foresee the future pages of your life turning towards your final chapter here on planet earth (meaning your transition), and then you can ask yourself: "What now?" Are the dividends of your life's discoveries enough to palliate your curiosity about why you were here and why you have to leave? Or do you now have questions about your energy identity, which is all you are going to be once you make transition?

For some, these are foreboding questions and ones they may spend a lifetime circumnavigating until they are impelled by fate to consider them. Why? Because of our investments in illusion, we have grown fearful of finding out the truth of who we are. But whose anxiety is this? It is not ours. We are already on our journey here on planet Earth to heal, learn, and grow. Somebody doesn't want us to know the truth. We are deliberately being kept in the dark. If you saw the movie *The Matrix,* you can begin to uncover translations to the spiritual message of this movie. It is symbolic of how we live our life. Facts on transition are the truth in all its beauty that we can embrace. How many dark days of worry can we refrain from once we truly understand the perfection of this natural, profound process? We are not mortals, after all, and all those repetitive and boring hours, days, months, and years we encountered had a spiritual significance, which we can now comprehend. There are far better opportunities ahead of us. We need to embody their understanding and our consternation about the unknown and trepidation about the future can become dismissed, along with our disquiet about death.

Turn your face to the sun and the shadows fall behind you.

—Maori Proverb

Recently I went to a funeral, my mother's actually, and at this funeral I had all but one of my siblings go through those depressing speeches about their mother having left them. I had a completely opposite feeling. I had spoken to my departed mother since her transition, made sure she had connected with her angels, and answered some questions she had. She answered some of mine, and I reminded her of what she knew (I had done my part to prepare her years before when her mind was lucid). By the time the funeral came, although she was there, she was truly unable to relate to most of what they were saying about her life. She had spent the last few years in a full-care nursing home, unable to recognize the people she knew and loved. She was now delighted to be where she was, and it was a rejoicing for her. She was a very active person who lost her sight and found this disability very devastating and limiting but was a few years short of turning one hundred, perhaps because of her consternation about passing on.

Depending on your age, you may or may not have witnessed people ending chapters of their lifetime and the apprehensiveness some of us can live around this natural event. For a protracted period of time in my younger years, it was one of my concerns until I learnt more about my own inner truth and its identity. No wonder I was afraid, because I was not living my purpose. I felt like a rudderless ship.

Perhaps when you reach transition, it is a little late for answers to those questions because your time on planet Earth is about to expire. The prospect to make constructive changes to your energy may be limited by time unless you experience divine intervention, but strangely enough, most people tend to only make enquiries of these—the most urgent and significant questions a person can have in their life—when they are looking transition (death) in the face.

If you can visualize when it is your turn, what are you going to do? Desperately hold onto every breath you take, hoping there are many more to follow, yet knowing there aren't? Grasping at life with distress and anguish because you believe there is nothing else or you worry you are going to fall into oblivion or because you demonize the unknown? How many people do this? Actually, doubtless many.

As far as we can discern, the sole purpose of human existence is to kindle a light in the darkness of mere being.

—Carl Jung

Perhaps this is too far in the future for you. Let us say your attitude about these scenarios may help decide providence because you have a force within you, uniquely yours, that decides your departure date (transition). This date, although you may support improvised ideas of influences, is actually derived from your attitude about soul-discovery, or more simply said, your response to your inner truth. We can further validate transition as the ultimate reward for a well-invested life, or it can be a security measure to help us avoid wasting our investments. In other words, cutting the silver cord to prevent us living trivia or because what we came to do we have completed.

This, your soul part, is more than a pleasant idea for you to play with. It has real control over your life and your experiences. You may therefore choose to deliberately join forces with it, have it at least on side, and make compromises with your whims and preferences, which are predominantly discordant with your purpose. Become more real about your relationship with yourself. After all, it is in charge of your fate.

We have a metaphor here for you to experiment with.

Envision that you are in a position of power, maybe a war office where your job is to keep secrets safe, but you are aware of how much the power you protect can destroy. Conceptualize the people you work for are going to destroy a country for financial gain. You can appreciate it will have catastrophic consequences. There will be a retaliation, which will affect your stability and enjoyment of life and that of your family, friends, and fellow residents.

What do you do?

1. Do you blow the whistle?
2. Do you play good employee and protect the secret regardless of consequences?
3. Do you be a good citizen and broadcast the bad decision, sacrificing yourself and ensuring it is changed?
4. Do you evaluate the decision unemotionally, share your concerns with your superiors, and get their facts? Maybe they

don't even know about it or they have another reason for their actions you have not been made aware of.

The only answer I would choose is really the last one. The main idea is to *negotiate*. This is what feelings do; they balance, discern, and strategize solutions. Find facts, and then if you feel an urgency to act in a certain way, find out more facts on the consequences of this. What will your reactions contribute to assist or harm? Then when you are comfortable with a plan, you instigate it and endeavour to protect yourself at the same time. In the meantime, the situation may have made a 180-degree turn, and you are a hero instead of being in prison.

For the sake of an education in energy, let us evaluate the other answers. The first is an emotional reaction, based on theories of right and wrong, good and bad, justice and injustice, but in reality, each circumstance we encounter has a far greater width span to discern than that narrow view. The second comes from a feeling of powerlessness, playing a concept of being a victim of life. There are very few highlights to be lived with this perspective. The third is an admirable reaction of using the power of our feelings to instigate change, but unfortunately, it may lack the necessary experience to be effective and can stimulate a martyrdom situation, which may or may not initiate the desired outcome.

> In the middle of difficulty lies opportunity.
> —Albert Einstein

The force you have inside you is like the power of a war office, but you are really in control of it. You may have given your power up to authority figures (your employers in the war office) who make decisions about your life for you. These authority figures can be interfering in your life purpose which is detrimental to your health and happiness. You have to find out the facts on the situation. Negotiate your way out of the arrangement with exactness and develop a strategy.

Suppose you were in control of this force that makes the most imposing decisions about your life. You could decide and plan your time here on planet Earth and live an alternative way. There are people doing this, and with focus, discernment and total commitment, it is very possible for you to do it yourself. This command of fate would change any unsettled attitude and offer us the possibility to joyfully relinquish life today, tomorrow, or in a decade or two because we know and understand the purpose of passing on. Welcome it as a well-earned graduation from one plane to another, and do as many of our ancestors did before us and people today at a heightened level of enlightenment: wittingly and willingly embrace it. In fact, possibly even design its time and instigation, which brings up other questions such as: Are we more educated and informed today in the twenty-first century than our ancestors were in ancient lifetimes? Do we know more about our fate hereafter? Are we really ahead in this age of literacy and fast communication in our awareness?

> Who has fully realized that history is not contained in thick books but lives in our very blood?
>
> —Carl Jung

Although we confidently presume we are, perhaps we are not after all. Over time we have physically lost our third eye, which helped us to automatically stay in touch with our true home in the universe. (Awakening is the first step in regaining it.) This loss may help promote our consternation of the future and our ignorance about who we actually are while contributing to our becoming extremely fearful of death.

> Then on the third day Abraham lifted up his eyes, and saw the place afar off.
>
> —The Bible

In the past, our third eye helped us keep savvy with our purpose for being here and the influences we attracted that may have supported us and those that did not. We had one eye turning inward, figuratively speaking, that was focusing on self and soul-discovery (coordinating with the big picture of who we are) and two turning outward (watching where we were going), involving us in the day-to-day routines of living on planet Earth.

Regrouping the reality of us almost losing this precious insight, we can passionately rethink our more recent mainstream processes of self-development or our education systems of the world and reinvent the prudence and enlightenment of some of our more sophisticated ancestors and those of our advanced fellow men. Instinctively, we can redesign our life opening possibilities for guidance to heal our past and become the self-sufficient soul we really are. It is the essential part of our mission, and we will be living a stereotypical existence till we actually do.

It becomes apparent the critical part of our curriculum has been left out, the part about our soul history and its accomplishments on planet Earth. After all, it is the sole purpose for being here to rewrite our soul history in a more plausible way.

Perhaps in recent generations, because we as a race have been busy reading about everything and everyone else, we have forgotten to journal our own personal journey. Where did we make other people's opinions about who we are more relevant than our own? It is perhaps little wonder we have archaeologists trying to dig for clues to our ancient history in all the parts of the world we have been. Even more recently in our civilization's history, it was natural for people to write their diaries of daily happenings and inspirations, eventually binding them into an autobiography. Many of these necessary self-discoveries have been superseded by other less opportune self-development pursuits.

> Many teachers will tell you to believe; then they put out your eyes of reason and instruct you to follow only their logic. But I want you to keep your eyes of reason open; in addition, I will open in you another eye, the eye of wisdom.
>
> —Sri Yukteswar

You may have begun your search a long time ago or have recently stumbled onto it. It really doesn't matter. A little bit of forethought from wherever it becomes available may serve you well. When in your life have you found veracity menaced you and delusion or illusion protected you? Never in all likelihood is going to be the truthful answer.

The reality is, whenever you are feeling anxious about circumstances that affect you, it will be because you do not have the relevant information necessary to induce relaxed and peaceful assimilation. Being factual keeps us solution oriented, and deception renders us confused, anxious, and inevitably emotional.

If you want to know more about your journey on planet Earth and subsequent graduation from it, the question that requires an answer if you are concerned about passing on is, who do you envisage to walk you through the process of transition? We have to reconcile spiritual realities and accept there is no one as qualified or competent as you to do this. And once you recollect how and can open your memory bank to your last successful incarnation and use this rationale to recall the procedures, it will become easy.

When you pass on, you have your angels, which is all you need. Certainly in my experience, when I have connected souls who have passed on with their angels, they respectfully request me to release them (they are presently held in a healer's body) because I am wasting their time talking and they have their new direction to attend to. It is a far cry from the confused and frightened soul they were before the connection when they were uncontrollably sobbing or egotistically expressing their concepts as if I needed their counsel or caution.

We are going to talk about this in more depth later. This journal will hopefully remind you of the truth of this process, firstly revealing your energy identity and then by reacquainting you with the communication of your guidance, your angels. This alone has the possibility of making your life here and beyond here all you desire it to be, rather than promoting anxiety by the absence of the guidance provided by your angels to help you unfold your truth moment by moment. Fear can make you rigid with your life, its adventures, its involvements, and your transition and therefore unable to enjoy it.

Perhaps in evading realities, you had been hoping someone was going to help you refine your old life and start a new and better one on the other side? (There are many old religious teachings somehow distorted over time by misinterpretation, which can support these idealistic notions.)

This is why you have a team of angels. They back you to be aware of your actions now and futuristically to enable you to reap the rewards you seek on the other side by managing your investments now. Anytime you decide to communicate with them, your life is usually, rapidly, going to be magically enhanced.

> Death is not extinguishing the light; it is only putting out
> the lamp because the dawn has come.
> —Rabindranath Tagore

Likewise as no one can help you, except your angels, you can't assist anyone else, unless, of course, you are advanced in your enlightenment and trained by Spirit to act as their representative in certain specific ways.

They set the bar for our participation. I have seen many people meddle in these metaphysical specialties with disastrous consequences when they are not trained in a proper spiritual system. To deal with confused souls, we must be "cleared" by Spirit for our own protection, which involves evaluating our tendencies over three lifetimes to be permitted to train for the opportunity to work with this service. In other words, the universe opens the curtain for those of us with the right intentions who have travelled the pathways of their truth and are ready to be of service in assisting the search of others. If at anytime we choose to be opportunistic, we will once again be denied its insights, and the universal truths will be closed to our discernment. In these circumstances, if we persist, we will be working with the negative energy and not Spirit, which will possibly give us misleading visual or auditory impressions. It is another universal spiritual law we cannot bend or break.

Besides, both you and all the people you know have all the help necessary to transcend, except perhaps the certainty of the right way to access it. Your whole journey here on planet Earth is occasioned to relieve you of impediments and replenish your energy with actualities and understanding. The moment is a powerful and potent episode in our life, and when we invest in it instead of being caught in the past and yearning to relive it or being tormented by its memories (negative replay) or projecting ourselves into the vast desert of the future, we can have momentous awareness of ourselves and our omnipotence, living in a stream of energy provided by our angels, which is miraculous. When we are in the shadow of their aura, we can relax and ignore all the trivial and emotional blockbuster concerns of our life.

To live our compassionate nature, we can offer our unconditional love and moral support for a person's final hours on planet Earth and help him or her relax with his or her transition, sharing our wisdom of predetermination. We can share with people about to make transition on the reality of their angels and the necessity to look up and signal their permission to be guided by them. This is a great service, and in gratitude, their angels may open the corridors of discernment for those involved to witness their transition.

> Grief is perhaps an unknown territory for you. You might
> feel both helpless and hopeless without a sense of a "map"

for the journey. Confusion is the hallmark of a transition.
To rebuild your inner and outer world is a major project.
—Anne Grant

This journal seeks to open passageways for you to uncover facts about:

o   Who you are
o   Where you come from
o   Where you are going

It will at least introduce you to the process of discovering and uncovering and help you learn the existence of the spiritual Internet where you can surf the spiritual web (metaphorically speaking) for answers. But like whatever new we learn, it has a certain language we have to master first. The explanation for this is shared under the questions and answers at the end of the book. The following poem demonstrates transition for us.

Vital of heav'nly flame!
Quit, O quit this mortal frame:
Trembling, hoping, ling'ring, flying,
O the pain, the bliss of dying!'
Cease, fond Nature, cease they strife,
And let me languish into life.

Hark! They whisper; Angels say,
Sister Spirit, come away!
What is this absorbs me quite?
Steals my senses, shuts my sight,
Drowns my spirits, draws my breath?
Tell me, my soul, can this be death?

The world recedes; it disappears!
Heav'n opens on my eyes! My ears
With sounds seraphic ring!
Lend, lend your wings! I mount! I fly!
O Grave! Where is they victory?
O Death! Where is they sting?
   —Alexander Pope, "The Dying Christian to His Soul"

Chapter Two: Immortality

*What we do for ourselves dies with us. What we do for others
and the world remains and is immortal.*

—Albert Pine

If you have ever wondered if someone is going to be there for you when
transition happens, you can now acknowledge this is the purpose of your
angels. They are always there. You have to look up. You will see them as
lights. When you call them in close to you, your whole perspective and
energy changes. It is the greatest miracle I have ever witnessed.

You may have had theories or dogma about all of this. If you are flexible
with new revelations, it may be time to discover if what you believed felt
factual or lacking some veracity or held only a snippet of reality or no
semblance of truth at all as you review it. You can now put it to the test
with a technique to help you be your own judge and jury of not only this
but to address solving any mysteries in life:

Technique #1: The Truth Echo Technique—the Echo of Your Feelings

Inside you there is a big echo chamber you may hear or see that is created for every idea that enters your realm of influence, and how loud or soft it is can help you monitor the truth. It almost happens at the speed of light, perhaps a bit fast to catch it at first, but you can dwell on it after the fact to help discover its message and authenticity.

To help you recognize it easier

o   Picture inside you there is a giant valley and as someone speaks his or her truth, it comes echoing back to you, or there is no echo at all or only a small one.

o   Now, using this innate quality each of us has (the echo), you can take each of the theories you have heard or lived, one at a time, and close your eyes and perhaps you will see the echo before you hear it, or you will hear it or feel its vibration or automatically as you close your eyes know the extent of the echo.

It is a technique suitable for many diverse circumstances. If there is an echo, it is the truth. No echo means it is false. If it is in between loud and no echo, there is truth but it is not being clearly presented for some reason. We can therefore call it a half-truth. Sometimes the reason we have no echo may be because of ambiguity or it is none of our business. Perhaps it is not our opportunity to be involved or we are ambivalent about the subject matter. If we pursue it, we may attract learning lessons we would prefer to avoid. Our souls constitution can guide us this way through our lives to make the right decisions once we are aware of its potential. We are, each of us, geniuses in hindsight; we can therefore use this for our educational purposes.

With practice using the Echo Technique, you can personalize your messages or communications with others to gauge their authenticity. In time its accuracy can become dependable. It will work better with the Clearing Technique #7 preceding it (refer to Chapter Five).

You may question where your inner truth and its constitution came from. We have journeyed extensively, possibly even to other planets, to reach the space we are in now, along the way we have amassed wisdom. If we can bypass our head where all our limitations lie, then we can access answers using our sagacity from eons of time.

There is considerably more we know than we could ever possibly conceive intellectually. It is essential for us to patiently feel our way through life, using our inner truth and its echo as our guide as opposed to thinking and analysing to make our decisions. Because the idea of this may be very new and foreign, it is necessary for us to familiarize ourselves with our inner truth because planet Earth is a strange and dissimilar world to our true home, and the more we settle in to its mass consciousness, the more difficult it is to extract the uniqueness of our own journey. We can acknowledge we are all really welcome here but as tourists. You can't reside here. You are just visiting, and in eternal time, it is less than a day trip. It is more like a second in time.

Are you having difficulty with this idea? At first it may seem a very strange concept. Perhaps it is best if we actually put it to the test. If you become sleep deprived, what happens to you? How long before you develop illness? Why do you require sleep? What happens to you when you sleep?

We come from an energy domain to planet earth, and as most alien movies depict, you need a recharge of your batteries each day to stay here. (These batteries are your energy centres in your body, which require an energy supply specific to its requirements to operate.) When you lie down and sleep, your silver cord, which is your soul's connection to home, stretches out to the universe, and you revisit home to recharge your energy. Part of this entails regrouping with your angels, which you may remember as dreams. In the morning, you feel refreshed and revitalized. If you did not make it all the way out for the recharge and instead became interfered with on the way, you may return tired and drained. This means that you have perhaps had a stopover in one of the confused zones. (This is explained in later chapters.) Over time this can lead to us compromising our immune system. We therefore need to relax before we sleep, clear our energy (Technique #7, refer to chapter five), and ask our angels to clear a passage for us to return home without disruption. Everything we desire we must request. Nothing is automated and our desires are then backed by the force of the universe. Now all this sounds like great material for an alien movie to me. These movies are yet another mirror for us to recognize who we are. Our true description is alien.

> Before the silver cord be loosed, or the golden bowl is
> broken, or the pitcher is broken at the fountain, or the
> wheel broken at the cistern.
>
> —Ecclesiastes 12:6

If you were living in your own home in the universe, your energy would be complete. Possibly the idea is new to you, but this understanding may help you be more prepared for the many more references to energy you will find in this book. That is what you are—intelligent energy, and everyone around you is identically constituted as intelligent energy. The intelligent part in no way refers to your intellect. It means your energy is wise, immortal, omnipotent, limitless and boundless, and it has many other qualities we will talk about, which you can recognize is not the potential of your intellect.

When you invest in your intellect, because it is made of planetary stuff, how will it benefit you if it is not really a permanent part of you? We can all resonate with the idea, Planet Earth feels like home. We are merely leasing time here. We don't own property of any nature, not even our body; it is therefore impermanent. One day the lease expires and you find a new place to call home or return to your real home permanently to regroup and then plan a new journey based on the results of your last one.

Reflecting for a moment, is there anyone you know who has lived here for longer than a century or two? The planet is three billion years old. You can conscientiously relate to people living for a century and a little more, but two? If it is our home, then why, we may wonder, can't we stay here, and why do we age and ultimately disintegrate through the passing of time? We may query why many of us want to stay beyond our time. When we accept the impermanency of this abode, we can ponder how long we will live.

> You must treat the days respectfully, you must be a day
> yourself and not interrogate it like a college professor. You
> must hear the bird's song without attempting to render it
> into nouns and verbs.
>
> —Ralph Waldo Emerson

We are investigating our intellect's mortality. This awareness can be confronting, especially since you are doubtless quite attached to it. In essence, soul-discovery permeates the realization your intellect, despite what you may believe to the contrary, is not even comparable to the best part of you. Presuming you have affection for your thinking mind, imagine how in awe you will be of your soul. As you become aware of your vulnerabilities, a whole new world of invincibility opens up to you. Consequently, it will become fundamental to learn some metaphysical truths to reprogram your intellect to respond to your inner truth, negating illusion's grip, thereby helping you live a very successful, peaceful, and contented life. Sounds amazing, right?

Our intellect is juvenile in comparison to the other nature we have. Therefore, conquering our inner dialogue with inner authority can assist us to shun influences that allow our thoughts to become caught up in following the wrong winds, as children tend to do when they do not have adequate guidance.

> The intellect has little to do on the road to discovery. There comes a leap in consciousness, call it intuition or what you will, the solution comes to you and you don't know how or why.
>
> —Albert Einstein

Using this as a metaphor, let us presume we don't give children sufficient direction or show true concern in our dealings with their self-education and development and instead cater to their whims. Then how do they guide themselves beyond our influence? We have essentially made life difficult for ourselves and for them because we have supported a misconception. Our behaviour has inadvertently misrepresented that life is going to cater to them, and despite their earnest endeavours to generate this, it mostly will not. Each time they are rejected or have a difficulty, they will come to us with their problems, which reflect a disappointing consequence, because their expectations were not met as easily as they were at home where their most impactful training for life began.

Our intellect requires direction, which needs to be regulated by our soul constitution, the "big picture" discernment of our lives and their opportunities. To find the truth in all mysteries for ourselves, we have this constitution and its blueprint for life to guide us. Similarly, we can call it our policies and procedures.

> We should not pretend to understand the world only by the intellect; we apprehend it just as much by feeling. Therefore the judgment of the intellect is, at best, only the half of truth, as must, if it be honest, also come an understanding of its inadequacy.
>
> —Carl Jung

As we evaluate our present awareness of transition with any new truths this book is presenting, it may help to find the symbolic nature in what life offers, such as games we can discover the rules of and/or to train for to enjoy. The following metaphor may assist with this process.

Suppose you went to play cards with card sharp people and proceed to invest money on your cards, despite being totally inexperienced, believing you have luck on your side. You are undoubtedly risking your financial assets if you pursue this. Why? Because you don't have the ability to strategize your luck, and your fellow players may lack integrity with your ignorance. Transition is the same. It is not as much a game but rather a game plan, but it does require proficiency or tools, as we can call it in a metaphysical vocabulary.

Walking into transition without having an adequate understanding of yourself is being put into a precarious position. Not everyone you meet on the other side will have your best interests at heart and the souls who don't can be the easiest to locate. Remember, the universe is home, but not all the suburbs are safe. Because you have no game plan and no GPS (refined sensitivity) to find your way and don't remember who you are and where you are going, you have an identity-crisis—we can call this spiritual amnesia. You are at the gateway to your real home, but you don't know where it is, and souls who are unscrupulous who have been in this void learning the art of confusion can take advantage of you while your angels are bound by spiritual laws that govern their inability to interfere. Not a win-win situation you may surmise.

We can likewise equate it with the circumstances of arriving in a big city renowned for its corruption and crime. How would you fare there without awareness of what is happening around you with all your possessions in hand and with nowhere to go?

Yet for centuries people (our ancestors), and if you believe in reincarnation, of course, we may be talking about ourselves in other lifetimes, have known all about what happens—and been prepared for it.

They may have welcomed it because they were well versed in the game plan and it was the final and total fulfilment of what they had been working on.

> Death is nothing. But to live defeated and inglorious is to die daily.
>
> —Napoleon

What happened to all this reality? Did someone forget to tell us? It is like a link in the chain of continuity was overlooked, and here many of us are living the end result of a giant failure of self-education. Yet don't we live in the education age? I guess it does not mean enlightenment. There are, of course, still some cultures that are presently practicing these abilities and making the most of their lifetimes today, but they are few. If you want to do a little recheck of this, you can evaluate how many people are working on placing their footprints in the sands of time in a meaningful way, living for the investments in continuity and not for momentary material gains.

> It is only when you are lost in your smaller selves that you seek the sky which you call God. Would that you might find paths unto your vast selves; would that you might be less idle and pave the roads!
>
> —Kahlil Gibran

You can read about these people in the newspapers, watch television (if you are brave and discerning enough to recognize the propaganda), or update with the news on the Internet.

How many people are there? You are bound to hear about it in this age of communication, because such people are rare, and we are guided by our inner force to resonate with their deeds of self-conquering and soul-discovery despite being unfamiliar with our own journey of truth. They first clean up their past, heal themselves, and then with time and good intention on their hands, make a difference to the ambiance of planet Earth by educating people about themselves. One person who springs to mind is Mahatma Gandhi. His actions are still inspiring and educating people today. He left his footprints in the sands of time for others to follow.

Be the change you want to see in the world.
—Mahatma Gandhi

Of course, there is plenty of dogma and theology begging notoriety, but it is not exactly what we are talking about, is it? There are plenty of people looking for fame and glory even through deeds of enmity, but what good is that? It is an empty vessel if we are not truly sowing a harvest of wisdom to deliver truth and freedom for others, and we will be forgotten with the turning of a page.

> The fruits of Christianity were religious wars, butcheries, crusades, inquisitions, extermination of the natives of America and the introduction of African slaves in their place.
>
> —Arthur Schopenhauer

In the past, some refined cultures prepared for transition and were not afraid of the process—because they knew life on either side of the dimension as a familiar friend. They invested wholeheartedly in their lifetime, overcoming intellectual incapacity and risking death without concern, in fact inviting it. They did whatever they could to conquer themselves, and in doing this, they were able to overcome their situations of repression. The story of the courage of Joan of Arc is another such inspiration. Their energy became unconquerable, impregnable, invulnerable, and insurmountable, which is more our true energy vibration, particularly when we have our angels around us and to attract them we have to live our truth and its policies and procedures.

In the interests of soul-discovery, perhaps it is time for us to evaluate who goes and who stays during transition. We are talking about our two natures. As for others accompanying us on our transition, I am fairly confident there are not going to be any volunteers willing to release their planetary opportunity to cross over with you or me and somehow keep us company on the other side before their time. Most people want to hang onto life and have enough self-loyalty to cling to their physical existence despite the departure of a loved one. And even if they do want to pass on at the same time, they will find it is a solo journey and truly unique in its destination, particularly if they are aware of their angels.

By now you may be thinking this journal is all about transition, and you may not want to read a book that is going to be talking up your death fears and prodding your anxiety about it—but really it is illuminating the opposite. This book is all about celebrating life and remembering how to live it in fulfilment in any dimension. But like the learning of any other game, we have the arduous task of learning the rules first, which makes it ultimately fun to play, and of course it is better enjoyed when we comprehend our objectives. If we look at the outcome of the game of life, the win and lose part of the game—the goals and targets one might have—transition (death) stimulates soul-discovery because it is the final score on the board of life, which dictates the pleasure of playing it. It is a big picture beginning of a new and more relevant energy opportunity.

> After your death, you will be what you were before your birth.
>
> —Arthur Schopenhauer

On planet Earth, if you do well in your training for a sport and excel at playing it, selectors of the bigger challenges/opportunities in the sport, the hierarchy, which we can call the professional league, notice you. It is similar to the message in the poem by Henry Wadsworth Longfellow:

> Lives of great men all remind us,
> we can make our lives sublime,
> and departing, leave behind us
> footprints on the sands of time;
> Footprints, that perhaps another,
> Sailing o'er life's solemn main,
> A forlorn and shipwrecked brother,
> Seeing, shall take heart again.
> Let us, then, be up and doing,
> With a heart for any fate; still achieving, still pursuing,
> learn to labor and to wait.

Life and death can be pretty like this too if you want to invest in yourself and train for it, so to speak. The selectors—we can call them this for the sake of the convenience of comparison—are really master souls sometimes referred to as messengers of God, angels, or Spirit. This is not a new idea because most traditional religions have alluded to them as being present with us on our journey. The master souls, we can say, are looking for people who did leave footprints or showed sincerity or lived their purpose. The big rewards are opening for them. Why would it not be? Whatever we invest in pays dividends in either energy expansion or repression.

The ones wanting to be saved and wasting time hanging out are not going to be in quite as good shape. They can be passed over and queue where the wait is pretty long and perhaps dismal. (I know this is going to trigger some dogma, but be patient. We are going to explain it all, and once you have the big picture, you can decide.) If you can trust these revelations are the truth, how important can they become to you? I know I was apprehensive to embrace it initially, but later I was sincerely grateful for the truth because it liberated me from the shackles of infiltrating concepts I was beginning to allow to nestle in and become comfortable with. Remember, we can change our mind at any time about how we wish to spend our time if we have chosen the time-wasting option up till now, and the after affect can be immediate. And sometimes through purging habitual self-condemnations we can rapidly become very elevated in our consciousness.

> The whole secret of existence is to have no fear. Never fear
> what will become of you, depend on no one. Only the
> moment you reject all help are you freed.
>
> —Buddha

Evaluating transition is an invaluable instruction for you to understand you, and if you never thought about life and death before, you really haven't touched on the big picture of yourself, your opportunities and the time to achieve them in. Time is always running its own agenda, with or without us. We therefore cannot afford to waste a minute of it. Remember, there is spiritual real estate of yours to redeem. How you invest in you determines how you travel beyond this lifetime. Your energy is your vehicle, and how rough or smooth it journeys its pilgrimages relates to your state of consciousness.

It is more difficult to plead complete ignorance to the process of evolvement now with all the great movies promoting some specific realities of transition. All of them have components of truth but none as yet have the whole truth, just like religions, which is why their message can be confusing to us at times. We often find it is missing some truth in the interpretation.

The purity of all the messages of the prophets, where most organized traditional religions sprang from, is I believe, without question the word of God, which related to his message specifically for the type of concepts and misunderstandings at the time it was delivered on planet Earth. They may not be as relevant at this time, or if they are, they may be more difficult for us to understand now because they are out of sync with our present planetary state of consciousness. Sometimes this can be because our interpretation has become a bit too intellectual to relate to the consciousness of the time, which has now changed.

Respectfully, we can acknowledge the origin of most traditional religions born millenniums ago, came from the word of God delivered for a specific people at a definite coordinated time, but in conceding this, we need to be flexible to update ourselves to the energy changes made since then. The prophets themselves did not just come once and tell one country or one people about God and his relationship to them. They came again and again. It surprises me that because of the narrowness of our beliefs, we cannot embrace the return of the prophet(s) we admired in another lifetime and in another culture. When you understand energy, it is easier to make this connection. Similarly fake prophets are easily identified particularly if they are preoccupied by sex, money or power. Many prophets chose a lone celibate journey to keep a clear channel with their angels. We can recognize people throughout their lifetimes by their energy, perhaps in a different culture always specific to the needs of the time and place. God has definitely never forsaken us; his word is forever defining as we refine. We talk about this in the states of consciousness.

> Leaders must fulfil three functions—provide for the well being of the led, provide a social organization in which people feel relatively secure, and provide them with one set of beliefs. People like Pasteur and Salk are leaders in the first sense. People like Gandhi and Confucius, on one hand and Alexander, Caesar and Hitler on the other, are leaders in the second and perhaps the third sense. Jesus and Buddha belong in the third category. Perhaps the greatest leader of all times was Mohammed who combined all three functions. To a lesser degree, Moses did the same.
> —Professor Jules Masserman, US psychoanalyst.

One fact we can rely on is that transition is an end of an era and the beginning of new opportunity. Well let's say, using another metaphor, you go to university, and the first day you are excited but nervous. You know you had to work hard to gain the privilege of entry. And now fast forward to look at graduation day. How well did you do? Have you got your degree? The ups and downs of acquiring it are in all likelihood forgotten in the final graduation. Putting your education to the test is what it was all about.

Life and after life combines similar elements too. We are investing in enlightenment and continuity. How well did we score? If we want to truly succeed at our graduation to the next plane, we have to allow our truth to invade all our realities. It's the main subject. We have to cram all the information of soul-understanding we can master into one little lifetime.

It seems an onerous task and definitely is more than a lifetime's work. (If you have been taking it easy, drifting along with the ups and downs, you perhaps don't have a feeling for it yet, but once you allow the engine of your inner truth to power up, all of this may change.)

Our hope of immortality does not come from any religions,
but nearly all religions come from that hope.
                                        —Robert Green Ingersoll

Before we leave this subject of transition, you may wonder how, if I personally have not had a near-death experience, I can be confident of this process. Some years ago, after my mentor passed on, I could feel the momentous change of energy that he and other angels, including those around me, were investing in the new millennium erudition, and because of my involvement in it the window was open for me to view it. I yearned to participate beyond planet Earth. Although I was educating people and being passionate about it, there was always that reserve that someplace else was going to be better and that place at this time was the universe. I embarked on an overland journey and was physically travelling by caravan, contentedly or as I believed living my spiritual purpose, and while I was regrouping my day's activities, I actually experienced a type of transition. I left my body and momentarily planet Earth. I believed my time had come (what other explanation could there be?). I had the magnitude of spiritual enlightened energy from my angels all around me. They questioned me on how I felt about making transition.

After a few moments absorbing this new dimension and its potentialities and pondering the strangeness of my predicament, I was healthy and very much alive but looking down at my body, deciding whether to return to it. I responded that it felt wonderful being here, but apologies for my bad manners, I was going to have to take a leave of absence on it temporarily because there were things I had not done on planet Earth. I had not realized until that moment the tremendous pull of those unfinished projects. My angels quizzed me about this decision before they allowed me to return, but I was certain this was definitely my decision. Almost in mid-sentence, an instant in time, I was abruptly returned to planet Earth, which felt like a crash landing, and my passion for being here has hardly wavered since. Needless to say, the window I was looking through observing the changes of energy closed and a new chapter on planet Earth began. This experience helped me to focus all my energy on what I was doing instead of being noncommittal with either place. The feeling of the tranquillity of transition lingered as the days, weeks, and years passed, but the yearning that bound me to my mentor faded and disappeared, being replaced by new and more exciting challenges.

To return to the experience of transition, just as those who travel in space have recounted, planet Earth becomes but a tiny spec in our reality when we make transition. We can feel returning to it is almost an imposition because we have copious opportunity in the universe to attend to. The less time we have already dedicated to our purpose on planet Earth, the more urgent our projects feel to set energy for a new incarnation to remedy this, which needs to be at least a seven-year investment of time. During this time we prepare our parents to receive us.

Spiritual Real Estate—How to Redeem It

Perhaps before moving on questions linger about spiritual real estate. The following explanation may help support your search for possibilities of this phenomenon.

Using a metaphor, imagine in this lifetime you have worked tirelessly and saved the money you earned going without luxuries because you wanted to achieve special investments for yourself. The money accumulates, attracts interest, and multiplies. What we are talking about is comparable to this, only it is energy instead of money, which, when you are enlightened and have energy "know how," is one and the same. Or in more intellectual terms, energy can be converted to money. Money alone cannot be converted to energy.

Spiritual real estate is your judiciousness of many lifetimes' investments. In more simple and understandable terms, you possess a certain talent innately, and it becomes easy for you to re-learn it this lifetime with an aptitude to become a skilled craftsman or engineer of a particular profession because you have done it before. And because it is so doable, you cannot accept that others can't apply themselves equally to the task. Your inherent talent is perhaps the result of a previous lifetime or lifetimes of dedicating yourself to this profession.

Some person or people in your background may readily recognize your capability and literally use you for it. Consider if you were employed because of your competency in this skill and as such you are paid for your time and the person employing you uses your talent unequally and makes a good business out of what you know. Although you feel appreciated believing you are acting as a valued employee, your employer can be earning all the money and you all the praise.

Maybe the whole business is built around your ingenuity and talent to train others. Let us presume your employer was lazy and ignoring his (or her if appropriate) life's lessons during his lifetimes, and his most positive venture was finding you. This is a small example of how spiritual real estate can work if we are not using it ourselves. We all have such abilities as we open more to our feeling memories, which we develop and refine. We can block them successfully with concepts of poor self-esteem or confidence, which just means we are out of touch with our feelings.

There is usually an inheritance of energy available to us in each new lifetime, a residue from the past. In other words, what we have built in energy remains for us to inherit when we return, but we have to remember it or discover ourselves to really redeem it. Living in our head is not going to produce it because our memory of it lives in our soul. It may have been accumulating if we have remained in an unawakened state for many lifetimes. When we clarify a past life we have had, particularly if it is publicly documented, we can recognize the talent that captivated others' attention or notoriety, and this can help us recognize our spiritual real estate. Because of the depth of my experiences backing others in their discoveries, I am confident all people have had a lifetime where they were exceptional in their achievements, which they can read references to. It comes with clarifying our real estate. It helps us with our present direction if we know our past.

Those already using their spiritual real estate you can recognize. They are in their feelings cruising through life, allowing success and happiness to be part of their existence, not blocking it with concepts or limitations. They may feel blessed in what they are doing (success happens easily for them and accomplishment seems assured), but they are mostly people who you are glad are successful because you somehow think they deserve it.

Before we leave the subject of spiritual real estate, it is prudent to concede we can return to the planet with a bit of an empty basket if we do not invest in ourselves and then the place of our birth, and the parents we choose can diminish in refinement. They will then in turn reflect the plundering of our spiritual energy, often through neglect and a decreased state of consciousness, which we lived in our last incarnation. We choose this because it helps to stimulate our loyalty and sincerity to break the bounds of our maze. We can participate energetically in our new family but with a feeling of not fitting in with their ideology for life. We know we are used to something better.

> We have within ourselves
> enough to fill the present day with joy,
> and overspread the future years with hope.
> —William Wordsworth

Chapter Three: Our Two Natures

Thoughts are the shadows of our feelings always darker, emptier ad simpler.

—Friedrich Nietzsche

If the revelations about our soul constitution sound unconventional, it is because the language is uncommon in our everyday life. It is challenging to explain a reality reaching beyond this physical plane in its derivation and for which we have somehow as a human race become generally oblivious to. But believe me, one masters it very quickly with desire because it is natural, after all.

We have two natures, ***one we feel with*** and ***one we think with,*** and they could not be more diametrically opposed because of our conditioning, yet both are intrinsically part of us. If we divorce one, it is like saying our personality does not belong to us or to disengage from the other; we are not ourselves.

When you try to equate which one endures and which one disappears when you pass on, you can begin to expose more metaphysical truths about your true self.

Isn't the real you the one you look at in the mirror when you comb your hair? The answer to this is really no.

The real you is your feeling nature, more invisible to the physical eye until it has developed the versatility to see beyond the physical dimension of life; the real you is well beyond the capability of your intellect to integrate its existence, but before we can embrace this idea, we have to begin at the beginning.

Our Feeling Nature

What is our feeling nature?

It is part and parcel of our soul part. We have been referring to this part of us as limitless, boundless, and immortal—here for the duration or what we call eternity. Our feeling nature can tune into all time dimensions, the one we are living now and the past and the immediate future. We may have to awaken it to this reality. It is where our inner truth lives, and it is how we communicate with the universe. And as we develop our spiritual refinement, our energy becomes even more defined than this.

If you are finding it a bit difficult to grasp, there is a good reason for this. You are conceivably trying to think your way through a revelation, which is unthinkable. Then how can you grasp it? We are going to break it down, and in time you can assimilate it because it is the truth. At least it's how your feelings work. It is where the echo lives in your feelings, which of course is the real you.

Our feelings can to some extent appear to go to sleep (hence our liberal use of the word awakened). As a metaphor, our feelings are like our computer, they go into sleep mode when we are not actually using them. To endeavour to identify experiences of this, we can say we become tired or bored when others around us are busy and we have nothing to do. We feel left out of the energy. We may yawn frequently and want to go somewhere else or daydream to escape the reality we are in. Our feelings are the same, but as they rekindle, they start to refine themselves. Depending on our energy at the time, this may be super fast or very slow and accommodating or somewhere in between. We cannot judge the suitability of this choice, whichever it is; rather, we can instead learn to trust it. Our constitution is exclusively all about the person we refer to as "me" which is a giant reality once we open the pages of the long forgotten past. But regardless of influences around us, we need to move as fast or slow as our feeling nature dictates.

You may have already started to think of feelings like excited, sad, regretful, remorseful, frustrated, emotional, etc. They are not truly representative of this nature; they are emotions, which are feelings of our thinking nature (our intellect). We can compare our true feelings to the ocean. It is symbolic of our impregnable nature being vast and invincible. The ocean is tranquil most of the time, not appearing to do much. It is nice and peaceful to watch if we are experiencing emotions. It can take a huge force of nature, like a storm, to move the ocean to show the real invincible power that is its potential. We are like this when living our inner truth. We are the same as the ocean, although it may be difficult to visualize on a bad day when we are all over the place emotionally. Storms are symbolic of alterations in energy. When we make a shift, we can become all stirred up, and once we have acclimatized to the changes, we are calm again.

Picture someone being offensive to the ocean and it rising up and running amok because it was emotional and displeased with what it heard. This is inconceivable and a stupid analogy because we can't relate to it. Likewise, it is unintelligent for us to become emotional about what others say, but we do.

If we can recognize the symbolic nature of this comparison, we can accept our true feelings don't often become aroused emotionally. We are immortal, after all, and don't need a body but have chosen one for a short time, therefore our true reality does not involve having anxiety about the dark or of being rejected or abandoned or other situations of this nature, and certainly not transition.

Accordingly emotions, because they are alien to our true nature, we can say for the convenience of learning, are invented. We inherit the habit of making them up, particularly from copying the behaviour of those around us or learning the concepts from our environmental influences in our first seven years. This is what we can refer to as our maze. We, our true selves cannot possibly be emotional in a confused way; it simply does not rhyme with omnipotent, magnanimous, immortal, limitless, etc., or at least not in my vocabulary.

Suppose we made the taming of our emotions our highest priority in life. What a transformation it would offer us. The challenge of this has perhaps rendered growing spiritually unpopular despite the amazing gifts it offers of insights, tranquillity, harmony, and intelligence.

> Pleasure can be supported by an illusion; but happiness rests upon truth.
>
> —Sebastien-Roch de Chamfort

This is why we can actually find people living inner serenity. They have switched sides when they began to find the tools to discipline their intellect and live life from their feeling part. For many this will be difficult to digest because emotions are now such stereotypical behaviour patterns, they have become the status quo, but we will explain this later in more depth.

Our feelings are the door to familiarizing ourselves with our soul part and its constitution. How we feel is our soul talking to us. There are multiple levels of sophistication that can happen with each occurrence available to us. Consequently, if we participate in emotionally out-of-balance behaviour, when we relax again, we can invite a regrouping of what we need to heal. We can refine this terminology later as it becomes necessary to do so. Our feelings have been since the beginning of time. All that we have done is stored in our memory bank that travels with our soul part. If we learnt about astrology in another lifetime, we can have less to learn about it this lifetime because we have already climbed that mountain of learning once before. We may be passionate to remember it again this lifetime, and we may suddenly have insights without reading a book or attending a lecture on certain aspects of it. We may have even written the book we are learning from.

If there is recorded history of our lifetimes, we may find we do the same things each reincarnation (e.g., become a politician, architect, lawyer, nurse, builder, engineer, teacher, person who cares for children, or doctor, make herb gardens, grow orchids, build cultured dwellings, collect real estate, breed dogs or horses, design things, paint, express ourselves in drama or theatre, or any number of things).

This is because it is a tendency of ours we brought from one lifetime to another. This can work for us or against us, depending on whether the tendency supports us or interferes with who we are. Some people have great difficulty deciding a career often because they have the past knocking on the door as the easy way and the future, offering a new and challenging alternative, but they may feel intimidated about beginning new adventures.

> What looks outside dreams; who looks inside, awakes.
>
> —Carl Jung

Our Maze

It may help us to learn more specifics about our maze. We can collectively say that it stimulates our desire to visit planet Earth. Because of the potentiality that our life's involvements here can present us with little realization of our true path and purpose, we can often chart the course of healing our maze over six lifetimes. If we revisit and do not make the necessary changes our problems are compounded and our maze grows longer and more difficult to navigate.

Our maze feels good; it doesn't feel like confusion at all because it is so familiar. This is why we call it a maze. We cannot easily find our way out of our habitual way of living. We acquire the roots of it in our first seven years, and symbolically our parents exhibit it with the dynamics of their relationships with each other and their and our relationship with our siblings. We can say we resume from where we left off in other lifetimes to continue to live the drudgery of repetition of this maze each and every day. We don't really know we are doing it. We can drift through life living this way without consciously acknowledging nirvana is within our reach. All we have to do to acquire it is change our attitude.

One good way to describe our maze is to recollect a memory of a recent tradition we participated in. Perhaps we celebrated a family reunion like Christmas and all our relatives came back home to rekindle family ties. Prior to our arrival, we are eagerly awaiting to reconnect with these loved ones and decide to dedicate a couple of weeks to prolong our involvement. Week one is wonderful. We are all happy with each other and eagerly sharing our news. In week two, however, the old familiar tension with members of our family returns and perhaps competition. Our parents may start acting as they always did, favouring one sibling over the other while endeavouring to pacify everyone.

We feel torn inside, but we put on a brave face and mature manner to deal with it remembering why we moved away from these entrapments. After compromising our truth, we return home grateful to be back at work, and it takes us a little while to recover from the painful elements of our Christmas traditions.

We have taken a journey through our past memories, and while this is therapeutic for us spiritually, we recognize areas of our life we have not healed. Our maze seldom triggers joyful recognition because we usually behave as a child again, thus allowing our amassed maturity to be disrespected by those from whom we personally desire acceptance and acknowledgment (e.g., parents). This can be because others (e.g., siblings) are perhaps leveraging for attention competitively and may encourage our exclusion. Why do we feel like this? It is because of habits. The soul part has no traditions. It is spontaneous, and it uses this nature to defy and limit the grip tradition can have upon us.

> Greater is he that is in you than he that is in the world.
> —John 4:4

Spiritually it is essential we outgrow being that little boy or girl who wants to return to Mum and Dad for nurturing. It is preferable that we rely only on our own nourishing of ourselves; this is maturity. We can then share our love unconditionally without having expectations of receiving praise or favour because we are insecure in our life without reassurance from others. This is why we chose our parents, for what they can show us we have done in past lives that we need to outgrow. It is then necessary for us to move beyond the limits of that background and go out into the world and learn new ways to live, and when we do return home, we will have copious amounts of newfound wisdom to share with our parents, thus fulfilling our part of the contract to obtain a body from them by educating them spiritually. This is continuity in balance. We grow beyond our early life and gain a greater wingspan than our parents. We can then in turn help them navigate their way through their maze. After all, we have become an expert on it. If we do this, we will be inspired and ready for the advancements our own children will offer us spiritually. Otherwise our children will initially need to reflect the state of consciousness of our parents because we have never grown beyond it and our lifetime continues to beg for its healing. When we mature, our children will have the opportunity then to heal and fulfil their destiny because we have done our part.

Although we will deal with explanations of our feelings in more depth later, we need to truly grasp some way to identify this part of us. It grows into the largest challenge we can have, to discern whether we are pivoting from our intellect or our feelings. Our angels only communicate to us through our feeling nature and in particular through using our primary perception (explained later in the book). There is joy, inspiration, and insight together with spontaneity and profound awareness we will miss out on if we are not cognizant with our feelings. Therefore, let us do a little technique that may help us discover more about them.

Technique #2: Identifying Our Feelings

o   If you close your eyes, there is darkness. Do you sense that into this darkness there is nothing?

o   Take your time to keep your eyes closed and maybe put earplugs in your ears to drown out the sounds of your surroundings.

o   Into this space, if you are alone, there are only your feelings, your angels, your intellect, and confused souls.

o   The first thing usually that comes into our mind is not necessarily our angels or our feelings. It is usually intellectual thoughts. This is where confused souls harass us, in these thoughts, and now we can familiarize ourselves with this invasion.

o   When we can distance ourselves from their influence and persevere in the darkness, we may slowly become aware of our feelings. We can ask ourselves, "What am I feeling?"

o   You may become preoccupied with intellectual ideas of feelings at first, being cold or hot, impatient, frustrated, or anxious. If you retain patience beyond these initial influences, your intellect may become bored with the exercise, and slowly your feelings can begin to communicate with you.

o   Because it may be a new idea, you may think you can't do it, but the truth is if you are unable to, it is because you have taught yourself not to; it is a natural response like thinking.

o   Consequently, you (need to) give direction to any voices that say you can't do it, using inner authority.

o   Since there is nothing we can't do, I have a little saying I use to give myself therapy: "Can't means I don't want to." Then I decide to do it or not do it.

o   Never compete or compare in this because it may take time to touch our feelings in a meaningful way. Humility and patience is where the power always lies.

As we will talk about in more depth later in chapter ten, our feelings are made up into four perceptions of communication. One of them is our primary perception. Accordingly, if our angels were to communicate through symbols, we might see a symbol over our third eye if we were a visionary. Through inspired thoughts that come with feeling, or maybe even a song or lyrics we might hear if we were an intuitive. It might come from an inner knowing if we were a prophetic and if we were a person of the feeling perception through our gut feelings. Gradually these inner knowings or feelings can have a sense of explanation. It may even last longer than our involvement in identifying our feelings. We may wake up in the morning with some explanations, particularly if we don't use an alarm to wake us up. As we open our eyes, answers to questions can be lingering there.

It can be a deciding moment for us to discover our feelings are a reflection of our refinement. In their evolvement, they are very layered and profound, like an immense body of water with endless opportunities for discovery. We can ask our feelings to do almost any bidding for us: train us, instruct us, bring information for us, travel through time to find answers to questions, show us how to love ourselves, wake us up without an alarm, communicate with others without words, read energy, or heal us. They are of course unlimited. Each day we open to the opportunity to use these dormant proficiencies. Suppose we spend our whole life on top of an ocean and never know what is in its depths. Worse still, conceive that you own the ocean and never discover its rich resources.

Why not make a resolution today to find out more about your ocean? Take up some spiritual diving techniques to help you find out what is in there. Don't be afraid of yourself. You already know who you are, and as you are that, why reject it? Our life rotates itself in circles, which means you will continually end up in the exact same place you are today if you do not expand your circle. When you return to this place, you need to have discovered many new shores for your ocean to wash upon. Then your regrouping will be as profound as you are. I want to say it is simple because it only depends on you. As there is no one else involved, you have the first and last say on whatever happens. Remember, you own the ocean. The following technique can help you exercise some of these realities.

Technique #3: Our Library

o   Use your Clearing Technique (#7 refer to chapter five) first.
o   Ask your angels for their backing for this technique.
o   Close your eyes and envision a library that you can go to anytime you desire for answers. It is your library.
o   Look around at all the books you have—they are wisdom gathered from eons of time.
o   Whatever you want to know, your librarian can organize answers for you in seconds.
o   Pause for a moment and consider this! With all this information available, what questions do you have for your librarian?
o   Ask them. Allow her (or him) to find the way to deliver you the information.
o   As you regroup your answers, did you see a picture, hear or read words, or have a gut feeling or an inner knowing.
o   Do you need more time to absorb the answers?

Your first angel—a very important presence in your life, usually assists your librarian.

Our Thinking Nature

Our thinking nature usually convinces us to allow it to run our life. This responsibility it really doesn't deserve because, as we have been qualifying, it is the new kid on the block in natures, only being born with our body this lifetime. It is poles apart from the refinement of our feeling nature. Whatever you were exposed to and allowed to train your intellect is what you are living with now. As we know, our feeling nature manages to resist participating in our life of trivia and becomes alert when it hears certain key truths.

When we incarnated this lifetime, we already had a very full and challenging life ahead of us without inventing other opportunities for our time here. Our thinking nature is frequently involved in fragmenting and diluting our real path and purpose because it is subject to outside influences. Consequently, we may be sourcing illusions to live in preference to living our designated purpose because it is more fun. All ideas alien to our purpose are illusion. As we think it, so it becomes.

Now you may be thinking you have not done this, but you may want to open yourself to its possibility because unfortunately, most people in Western cultures consider it a way of life. There are only very few people who have mastered self-attainment and have control over their emotions.

> Our heart glows, and secret unrest gnaws at the root of our being. Dealing with the unconscious has become a question of life for us.
>
> —Carl Jung

As a little self-test, ask yourself, "How much joy did I reap from today's investments?" And consider how much fulfilment you enjoyed from the opportunities of the day—how much contentment did you live, and was it all day or a small part of the day?

If you had stress or frustration, impatience, anger, agitation, irritability, or any other of those normal by numbers but abnormal by nature emotional states, even excitement, you will become disqualified from the membership of the self-attainment club or more appropriately termed those with higher states of enlightenment. Subsequently, if you did not live a high percentage of the feeling states and lived instead the emotions, you too may be living your thinking nature predominantly in lieu of a balance between your feeling nature and your thinking nature. This balance, when achieved, can design a joyful, fulfilled life. It is good to remember your feeling nature sponsors your thinking nature for one lifetime only.

If you want to belong to such a state of consciousness, the joy and fulfilment one, your life can be predominately calm, spontaneous, joyful, tranquil, fulfilled, and all the other feeling states that come into being when we have conquered ourselves.

> It is dangerous to be right in matters on which the established authorities are wrong.
>
> —Voltaire

You can do this following technique to put yourself in your feelings. It may not work at first because we are a little clumsy with new ideas but as you refine it, you can develop your own technique to make it work for you.

Technique #4: Sense, Organize, Act—a Way to Uplift Your Energy

o Using a fast pace, clap your hands in front of your chest, elbows bent and hands close to your chest. As you do this, say the word *"sense"* aloud.

o With the palms of your hands open gently touch your left hand on the left side of your head and your right hand on the right side of your head simultaneously and say, *"Organize."*

o Then push your hands, palms facing inwards, to clap with arms outstretched in front of you at chest height and clap your hands and say, *"Act."*

o Do this again and again until you gather a rhythm and your energy builds a feeling of elation and enthusiasm. Increase your speed of movement and the volume of your voice. This is a good technique for those days your energy is less than par. It can reenergise it.

As an additional tool, you can, when you become proficient at this technique, at the end of it keep your hands together momentarily stretched outward and point them at whatever you want to manifest after you have said, "Act" an imaginary visualised target or goal. The point that you give your energy when you have your arms outstretched in front of you is very significant. When our energy is focused, it has a point. When it is asleep, it is rounded. This is why we awaken to enable our energy to begin refining and showing up in strength to back what we are doing. We need to give our feelings opportunities for involvement in every moment of our life or they will quickly return to 'sleep mode' as our computer does.

If you are applying for a job or you have a pivotal appointment in business, a meeting with the school, or any other such challenge involving others, you can do this technique prior to going there and your energy can reach a peak where you can feel you can accomplish whatever you truly desire. People automatically respect us when they feel our energy is high. It is a subliminal consciousness we respond to. It may not mean you will succeed in your job application unless it is the right one for you, but you will perhaps feel out-of-balance emotions of others and their thoughts about you that would normally affect you adversely and with the heightened energy now be able to remain detached even intrigued by your own sensitivity and its insights. Always exercise patience with yourself in learning new ways. Our feelings absorb gradually because we have incredible depth; nothing is shallow with them. We can therefore assimilate new realities and automate them (and turn them into an aquatic life if you like the metaphor of the ocean), and this takes time. Whatever negativity you hear about yourself from your internal dialogue (thoughts) is an effort by confusion to try to sabotage you, which you are going to learn about later. Therefore, patience is the answer and even more patience when it runs out.

Chapter Four: Loyalty And Sincerity

*Unless you can find some sort of loyalty, you cannot find unity
and peace in your active being.*

—Josiah Royce

If you want to reach attainment, and acquire inner peace, fulfilment, and
harmony, not to mention all those limitless virtues we have already referred
to, there are specific qualities to foster to help you facilitate this.

To climb the ladders of enlightenment, there are two loyal soldiers
who can escort you: they are *self-loyalty and sincerity,* and of course
accompanying them is a desire for the truth. Other qualities appear along
the way, but these two are what turn the key in the ignition, ignite the
engine to commence the journey. If you like to break it down, self-loyalty
is the key in the ignition and the purr of the engine, and sincerity is
putting it in gear ready to go. It's pointless going anywhere on foot because
you will soon run out of energy if you want to cover a large landscape of
evolvement.

As you decide if you want to take this journey of soul-discovery,
you may already be thinking, *Who can I take with me?* The response is

an unequivocal: no one. You may protest at this, wanting to enlist the company of loyal friends or loved ones. The truth of being unique has to be understood comprehensively. Whatever you do for yourself will not have the same impact on others, and this may be the result of many considerations, not the least of them being timing, regardless of our belief in their readiness for change in their life. This is the first challenge of instigating self-loyalty, realizing the solo nature of each of our journeys.

You and your soul part are ready for the direction you are about to undertake, and others may either not be ready for what you are doing or have previously put their hand up for other opportunities. If you pressure them to change course, they may do it to please you, and it will only disappoint you eventually when they are inclined to, metaphorically speaking, skip off the ship, drag the chain, or even perhaps overtake you, which may make you feel inadequate. It comes back to possessing those two qualities, starting with self-loyalty—which means you are committed to your own true desire first and its destiny second.

It appears to leave only a third-rate type of concern for others and their spiritual undertakings, and that is the way life at the awakening level works best. Otherwise you may manipulate yourself to wait for them to share at your level or worse, try to compete with them. If you are focused on your own commitment to yourself, you will meet people on the way, possibly even loved ones from this and other lifetimes, you will have affinity with. They are on the same journey as you, and they became motivated by their own self-loyalty and sincerity. You may have copious notes to compare with them. They chose the same ship you did and don't want to alight because it was their idea in the first place; no one pressured them. Those you meet and have affinity with are your spiritual family. They have usually been around you longer perhaps than your earthly family, even though you only recently met them. To reconnect with your spiritual family can be the most liberating addition to your life because they do not require explanation for your reasoning. Often nothing much makes sense about our life, or there is little depth to it, until they appear, and this usually coincides with finding one's spiritual path and purpose.

All of the above momentous changes happen in energy. You have not left home, changed jobs, divorced, or changed your routine. All you did was change your attitude to yourself and empowered your angels to take care of the rest. Those around you in your place of employment may recognize your change of attitude and begin to engage you in sharing your discoveries. It may be timely to realize the reason we are not a prophet in our own household or town may be because people who know us well may be resistant to accepting a more-refined version because it invites pressure for them to follow our example and they may be unable or unwilling.

> It is wrong to think that love comes from long companionship and persevering courtship. Love is the offspring of spiritual affinity and unless that affinity is created in a moment, it will not be created for years or even generations.
>
> —Kahlil Gibran

Your spiritual family may be scattered among your earthly family. They will be the ones you feel the most relaxed with, particularly once you change your attitude to yourself. At least one or more of our children are part of our spiritual family, and if they are not, they will be part of our partner's spiritual family. Because when we come to planet Earth, our first priority is to heal karmic situations with our supposed enemies (in actuality there is no such relationship—our love nature is all-encompassing and unconditional), we often choose them as our earthly family to enable us to return to a love situation with them again. Of course, if we give an excess of energy to hate, it has to be love disguised as contempt because of disappointment through some kind of failed relationship. The real opposite to love is indifference. It is why we hear many people wanting to make a difference to the world, and they use these words because they want to share their love with their fellowman, and this will make the greatest difference to mankind when they do.

Our spiritual family we mostly have already returned to a love situation with, and they can therefore be very supportive of us instinctively. Thus it is wise to open ourselves to all prospects, as we are unlimited. As we grow in enlightenment, the less we desire other people to support us and the more capable we become. We don't share our intimacies with many others because it isn't necessary. We become satisfied with good, quality fellowship with other souls (regardless of gender). We can open to a bigger picture of sharing soul to soul rather than being caught in the trivial judgment of people by appearance, money, race, gender, or other limiting points of view, which can captivate us in a small picture.

> Love others as well as you love yourself.
>
> —Jesus Christ

This is why it is called freedom. All the old baggage we can leave behind us as we transcend to a greater consciousness. Picture yourself having the freedom to love all souls with unconditional love, accept them where they are at spiritually, and be open and aware of what is your opportunity. Loving people unconditionally does not mean you have to perform some deed or sacrifice for them, but if opportunity knocks, at least bigoted or racial ideals will not block or inhibit a profound involvement life may offer you.

I would like to share an incident involving my daughter. When she was only six years old, she moved to a very small school with an attendance of about seventeen. She wanted to have a birthday party and invite the whole school. We had a large property with many resort-like facilities. It did not present any problem if many came. At the school there were children of a mixed race. It never crossed my mind that this would present problems.

As the party progressed, it seemed like the whole village was there, and we were meeting most of the parents for the first time. Then my daughter came to me, distressed and crying, and told me her best friends were absent and she could not enjoy her birthday without them. I asked some of the parents if they knew why the children did not come. Firstly I was told they didn't have a car, to which I responded I would pick them up. Then I was told the children lived in town, which was about thirty minutes away. I travelled twice this distance at least twice a day, it therefore presented no problem for me. Finally I was informed they did not have a phone, so I asked if there was a neighbour I could ring. It was only at this moment I learnt they were indigenous and would not come anyway. Now how was I going to explain to my distressed daughter that they had actually refused to come to her party because of the colour of her skin?

Therefore, in a very tactful way, I attempted an explanation of considerations here, perhaps cultural differences her friends were sensitive to. She was agitated and did not accept anything I was telling her. I suggested to her as an example that perhaps the colour of their skin may be darker than hers and this had made them feel reluctant to participate because the people here were dissimilar. "No," she exclaimed, angry at me for suggesting there was some type of difference between her and her friends. "They have the identical colour of me," she said, pointing to her arm. She was emphatic about it, although she had an English complexion, complete with chalk-white skin. She never saw any distinction, which was very reassuring to me as a parent. We had unconsciously delivered a more advanced spiritual education.

I promised her we would ask them if we could have a second gathering with them, which was the only way to console her and have her return to her party to enjoy it. They remained good friends with my daughter through the years, notwithstanding a couple of years after her party she changed schools again. She often visited her old school walking in like she owned it and demanding to be included in their activities. As adults these children protected each other when racial issues arose amongst others in each of their additional circles of friends. Today she enjoys extraordinary advantages because of her big picture spiritual attitude. It has opened many doors for her to help people spiritually—She walks right through others' prejudices trampling them on her path and has amassed an extraordinary following. Her loyalty to her inner truth is absolute.

> Our loyalties must transcend our race, our tribe, our class, and our nation; and this means we must develop a world perspective.
>
> —Martin Luther King

Sincerity Overview

The other quality, sincerity, manages to pull us through rough patches, which usually manifest with the rediscovering and owning any particles of lost truth. If we meet our friends or loved ones on the same journey, then we are fortunate, because for that length of time we share the same space, we can communicate with them perhaps in a more relaxed and fellowshipping way. We can evaluate them more fairly as a soul travelling their unique journey instead of having expectations of them, which can be very healing for everyone.

Then we may reach crossroads again. Perhaps our paths may go in diverse directions and then sincerity comes to the forefront again to help us hit the accelerator. In those times, it is imperative to trust the forces that are within us and supported by those around us who know better our direction than we do at that moment. They usually always do. This search for self-understanding is aptly called Awakening.

Awakening

That is the first stair we step onto in our ascent. If we reach the acquisition of self-attainment we are talking about, we will be in a heaven on earth. Whereas we may think of life more as a hell-on-earth at the moment, particularly as we pursue other feeling options readily available to us, such as meditation, and we realize that life in its natural nature feels like this. We may realize how much we have left "me" out of our lives and how empty an existence we have lived because of it. Or we may be unaware there is a choice to what we are living.

> I sent my soul through the invisible
> some letter of that afterlife to spell;
> and by and by my soul returned to me,
> and answered, "I myself am Heav'n and Hell."
> —Omar Khayyam

If we have an emotional life, it is a hell that is unnecessary for us to live; hopefully situations will change for us along the awakening way. Of course it will depend on the commitment of ourselves and the influence of our two loyal soldiers, self-loyalty and sincerity.

If you are wondering what to expect, it is not wise to have expectations of our selves then we won't be demanding what we are not ready to feel. It is a journey, not a destination, and discovery can happen daily, weekly, or monthly. Sometimes it may only be a yearly event for those who lack self-loyalty. We may only really consider this, the presence of one's soul, when we go on holidays which helps us to change our backdrop and relax. As with all of life's adventures, it depends on how much energy we invest into learning about ourselves as to the dividends it remunerates us with.

Maybe in the beginning you may participate as a spectator. It's always up to you. If the road gets rough, take a break, put the book down, and wait till you empty out and develop a thirst again. You can educate yourself to be your own spiritual physician since there is no one who knows you like you know yourself. Because you are a soul, it is a long-term investment. As a soul, you really are very self-contained and have your own self-diagnostic tool within. Sharing from the pivot of involvement with many people growing spiritually, even if you hit a rough patch of inner truth discerned, never, ever give up on yourself, not even momentarily. Within you there is beauty profound and unique which the universe desires you to return to and of course planet Earth requires it more. It is awaiting its inauguration.

> The more a person analyses his inner self, the more insignificant he seems to himself. This is the first lesson of wisdom. Let us be humble, and we will become wise. Let us know our weakness and it will give us power.
> —William Ellery Channing

Life is like a giant mosaic, and each of us has our special piece of sophisticated philosophy or erudition essential to its purpose we collectively need to add. As with anything precious and pure, it necessitates careful handling and patience to allow it to unfold in its own timing. Imagine if your unique vibration was all about forgiveness. You have come to planet Earth to allow forgiveness to unfold first with your own self-attainment of it and then you can acknowledge the planet generally has been operating without clemency and compassion, blaming difficulties on individuals instead of taking the bigger picture perspective of forgiveness. Prior to this revelation, somehow your inner truth was contaminated with programming and you were living the opposite of forgiveness. You then open to live your constitution, and as you do, at first you notice those around you becoming more compassionate to each other. Then as you grow in energy, this goodwill spreads beyond you to the city you are in, and as you clarify it even more, clearly it affects a further and wider circumference of souls, cities, etc.

This is how energy works. If we really want to grow spiritually and gain self-attainment, we have to invest courageously in ourselves. That is going to mean no self-judgments, no self-criticisms, no self-abuse, verbal or physical, or at the very least a resolution daily to change any habits that can make us do this to ourselves. These bad habits can delay our self-attainment.

Playing a victim of life's circumstances overwhelmed by adversity or of others in our lives is a very provocative confusion we can be captivated by. Unfortunately, the other end of the seesaw is being an abuser, which is prejudicial to our innate love vibration. Hence it is preferable to find the middle path, which is balance, a balance of thought and feeling. It is good to realize in these circumstances we have a power within that is invincible greater than any outside force, so when we relax, we can use our potency and our angels can empower us to heal our misunderstandings to evolve beyond this low level of consciousness.

You are a precious piece of the universe that requires reverence and respect. That's what loyalty is all about, demanding a change in circumstances that previously rendered you less than omnipotent.

As an example of showing loyalty, we can take a very overused situation but one that offers us good insights. If there are only five slices of cake and six people present, are you going to be the one who will go without? First you can ask yourself, do you want a piece of cake, (is it in your best interest to eat cake—yes or no?), and if the answer is yes, it is not your opportunity to miss out. Speak up for what you feel before you become emotional about it and then try to suppress it.

Hiding emotions is unhealthy. Therefore, your attitude is injurious to you when your inner truth may be demanding a voice and because your intellect has an opinion based on your education about etiquette, undeserving concepts, or any other ideas that provoke this behaviour, it is suppressing it. Request that the cake be cut again and then everyone will enjoy a piece, or allow someone who prefers to avoid eating a piece to speak up because you had the courage to lead the way, which is more likely to be the outcome.

This is the first lesson of loyalty. It will become a fundamental necessity to change the way you think. You apply the cake lesson to many circumstances of your life. This is a good beginning. There is a technique you can do to help your loyalty become more predominant in your life. Remember, this is one of the early steps after awakening to consolidate before we can truly move to anywhere more peaceful on our journey. No matter how far advanced you are in your quest for enlightenment, this technique can facilitate filling any cracks in the foundation of your energy. It assists our avoidance of self-manipulation.

Technique #5: Self-Loyalty—Redeeming the Soul Focus

Me first, me second, everyone else third

o   Stand with your feet shoulder width apart, arms by your side.

o   As you slap the palm of your right hand on your chest, say, "Me first."
o   As you slap the palm of your open hand on your chest a second time, say, "Me second."
o   Say, "Everyone else third" as you bring both your arms pointing away from your body near shoulder height.
o   Do this several times until you feel its strength.
o   Use a loud voice and a firm hand slap, showing your inner authority.
o   You can, if you are having trouble with your loyalty with any particular person, say, "Me first, me second, and the person's name third."
o   Check your voice, tone, etc., to make sure it is strong and meaningful.

After you do this technique several times, you will feel differently about your life. You will feel stronger and more directed. Others can similarly benefit because you can become more reliable and forthright in your life, which makes everyone who may depend on you feel more comfortable with your new strength.

This is a very potent technique and one you can use many times, if you have trouble with loyalty, until it becomes automated in your feelings. For those who are having difficulty with the concept of self-loyalty, the following explanation may help you to open yourself to considering how you need to be the king of your world. The explanation is lengthy because this is one of those stumbling blocks we can't bypass but must go through. It is the first step for some on the awakening threshold to spiritual enlightenment or maybe the stumbling block they keep falling over as they navigate their way through the states of consciousness but can't quite consolidate.

You may wonder, as others before you, why we suggest this technique and be concerned it is encouraging a selfish attitude. To allay such concerns, particularly if we are robotic in our attitude to life, (it means you perform deeds out of duty instead of desire, being loyal to dogma at the expense of yourself and whoever you involve in that idea) we can explain it further. Some of the most notorious criminals we have read about in the news have been robotic in their narrow perspective. They can't feel what they are doing because they are in a programmed state of mind. They act out of a system of learned behaviour, believing it is their duty, and cannot feel the consequences of their actions. They are numb because their heart chakra is blocked.

> Loyalty to petrified opinion never broke a chain or freed a human soul.
>
> —Mark Twain

The "me first" technique is all about our energy (where the real estate we want to reclaim lives). First we are loyal to our feeling nature (the invisible one). The "me second" part of the technique is being loyal to our thinking nature, which includes our body. To offer an example here, have you ever wondered why you put an oxygen mask on yourself first on an airplane before you attend to children or others? It is the same principle— you are then assured of being efficient in caring for those who may be depending on you, whereas if you are gasping for breath, you are going to be preoccupied with breathing, thus delaying a solution for yourself and those you wish to take care of. It is simple common sense really.

It is like doctors and nurses. They can't show up unannounced at a hospital one day and say they would like to look after sick people as a doctor or nurse; they have to go through a training process first to be qualified. Along the way, other people evaluate their suitability for the opportunity in case they made a mistake in their choice of profession. We can't help others if we are spiritually incompetent. What makes us qualified? Step one is loyalty to self.

Hence, we have to comprehend how we operate internally. What is involved in being a person like ourselves? We have to become credentialed at running this universe of ours first before involving ourselves in other preoccupations. These are the spiritual prerequisites for branching into spiritual educational involvements with others. When you can respect your own energy and its ability to self manage then you can likewise automatically respect and support it in others.

When we become efficient at helping ourselves first, building a strong pivot point for living our life here, we can help others spiritually. It may be part of our future or our real purpose, but we can't run before we learn to sit up, crawl, and walk. It is the process of self-development. No step can be overlooked if success is to be assured. Sharing what we are experiencing ourselves is not meddling as long as we avoid giving advice. The best way to share is begin with, "In my opinion."

Another example of disloyalty is when we attempt to rescue someone if we are not equipped or skilled adequately either spiritually or physically. The following metaphor may help define this for us.

When we attempt to save someone drowning, despite being unable to swim, the consequences can be disastrous. Instead of one person seeking help, we have two people drowning. A person on land can find assistance. There are options: skilled help, boats, life rafts, surfboards, or any objects that float. Once we jump into the water, we lose many of those intelligent options open to us and take a dutiful (robotic) step, which can make us drown.

Are you convinced about the importance of self-loyalty? It is a tough spiritual truth to grasp. It is really being intelligent and focused in challenges that befall us. Taking the drowning example further, it is easy to envisage other consequences if perhaps a person involved in this has five children depending on him/her for their support in life, and when this person drowns trying to save a stranger, we can easily appraise in hindsight how intelligent it was. The outcomes could be far reaching on the five children. Was the desire to be a hero and attempt to save a stranger but instead perishing, intelligent?

If we are a strong swimmer, we become grateful for the opportunity to be able to support others with our expertise and the fulfilment of its success one can live with for a whole lifetime. We are loyal and qualified in these circumstances to our true desire to exercise our compassion in the service of our fellowman. We can say the same spiritually.

> In thy face I see the map of honour, truth and loyalty.
> —William Shakespeare

We can use less extreme examples of a lack of loyalty when we dilute our energy through favouring a preoccupation with catering to others, giving up our valuable time for their whims. There may be favours they want us to perform for them at the expense of what we want or need to do for ourselves. We can observe this daily as people readily share them as their way of life, proud of their sacrifices. It is necessary for us to evaluate each circumstance on its merits. To do this efficiently, we process our options with detachment from others' opinions or even our own and follow our gut feelings. There are always solutions to predicaments that harness our time negatively. In finding these, we grow in stature and leadership.

A bigger spiritual picture of working with others we feel obliged to help who can be loved ones is to recognize their potential to meet their life's demands confidently may even exceed our own or be at least equal. No one is lost, and everyone has angels, which, when we know better, necessitates us adopting a different and more expansive attitude to others, encompassing their free will to make their own life experiments. This allows us to take a step back and really discern what our opportunity is and what is meddling. Loyalty is the first hurdle we have to scale in our quest for enlightenment.

If we try to interfere in other people's lives or attempt to solve their problems for them, even though we are not in this line of work, we are perhaps even contributing to their stagnation because we can make them weak and incompetent by intruding in their decision-making and/or direction. We can mistakenly presume it is necessary to give them advice when in reality this is interfering. We can do this when we have an opinion, they need our help, or it is our duty, or worse, we want to be needed. In these circumstances, we indiscriminately keep others dependent because we need someone to save to feed our ego.

When we know better, we can learn we have enough responsibilities of our own to fulfil. Sharing our insights with others in a detached way is an empowering experience. If we take it to a wider perspective, we may begin to notice dogma or lack of loyalty can be a very dangerous preoccupation because whole communities of people can be living dutifully out of their own self-control, thinking they are doing what they should be doing, honouring their obligation, but are they really? When playing a role where priorities reign instead of intelligent energy decisions, we have to question who is really running their universe if they are not running it themselves. It is a very scary thought. No wonder we are obsessed with locking our doors at night.

> Every form of addiction is bad, no matter whether the narcotic be alcohol or morphine or idealism.
>
> —Carl Jung

With our own inner truth on board, we can be loyal to it, and it will direct us accordingly. This is a protection for others, because in a challenging situation, one can count on those with self-loyalty to protect one's interests as they protect their own. In other words, they would act intelligently in all circumstances. We may believe we want people to cater to us, but this nearly always produces disasters eventually.

A dog is a symbol of loyalty. To explore this as a metaphor, speculate buying a dog that is not loyal to you and is playing the role of super dog with all the neighbours who don't have dogs. It is attempting to guard their properties, eat their food, play with their children, and keep them company in their car. How would you feel about sharing if you really want the dog to be with you? Instead the dog is busy catering to everyone else.

> A dog is the only thing on earth that loves you more than
> he loves himself.
>
> —Josh Billings

It is okay to help people if they ask us and we really want to—then there is energy for it—but to devote ourselves to others at the expense of our own desire to live our purpose is not conducive to the happiness of either person. This may make us become resentful because we can't do what we want to do and the other person or people can become dependent because we have taken opportunity away from them to discover their own solutions and to grow in the confidence of learning from their own mistakes. They can become dissatisfied and may demand more and more. There are always solutions available to benefit all parties to change circumstances making us live outside loyalty. Consequently, loyalty to self works for everyone.

Before we move beyond loyalty, it is necessary to say this is a first step for winning back our energy and putting it in a focused format. It is at this level of awakening and through to the seven steps of acknowledging ourselves as a soul and living this priority that we emphasize the importance of loyalty and sincerity.

As we scale up the levels of enlightenment, contaminated and/or limited focuses can change if we put the effort into the foundations of self-loyalty successfully. In the first level, we have to learn about *"me,"* which is explained further on in the states of consciousness. Because most people generally miss many of the steps in the awakening process without a refined system of awareness to follow, we need to consolidate the tears or gaps in our aura at some time.

In my experience, this whole loyalty to self pathway does not initially engender comfortable participation because it is moving our goal posts to a place more difficult to reach. Once you stretch your aura to these new heights, you can be transformed into a very special being with a great deal of integrity, not only with yourself but with others as well. This is not an opportunity to be squandered.

Sincerity

Although our experiments with sincerity spiritually may be limited, we can describe them as using tenacity to break through obstacles that present themselves in our spiritual path with self-control and self-discipline. Subsequently, in the face of the truth, which can be confronting, we have sincerity and integrity within ourselves to keep our search moving forward, regardless of the consequences or changes we have to make in the way we think. Sincerity gets the job done.

We love people who are sincere with us because they are always supportive and help facilitate our success. Sincerity to self is self-support and making changes happen at the expense, if necessary, of rejecting others' plans for us. If you can acquaint yourself with these two loyal soldiers/ qualities, you can begin with more earnestness. Up till now, we have only been sharing probabilities. The real journey is still before us. We have levelled the energy or reached a space where we have enough language we can relate to and the possibility opens to advance more courageously with our inner truth and the content of our soul's constitution. As we do this, we will divulge the same truths already shared with a greater depth. This is how our angels guide us in all situations. They open the door a little, and when we have absorbed our revelation, they expand its opening, enabling us to take an even wider perspective without becoming overwhelmed.

> Wisdom is not a product of schooling but of the lifelong attempt to acquire it.
> —Albert Einstein

A Cautionary Note

At times if we are fixed in our ways, the road from here sometimes moves through hostile or unknown territory, and it is therefore going to appear unpaved. But if it gets a bit too tough, or you can't concentrate or absorb the information, put the book down and take some R & R time away from its revelations, which are the result of years of concentrated and determined tenacity to reveal metaphysical truths. It is hardly light reading material for most.

You are essentially full and you need to empty. The best way to empty out is to share with someone what you are feeling (it doesn't mean to seek advice, because no one knows your journey; it is only yours alone). No one can possibly even begin to understand what you are feeling because others are not you. You are unique, and your decisions are made in accordance with this individuality that makes up who you are. You can preferably share with someone who is a good listener rather than a good talker. Then you will feel empty and resolve again to involve yourself in discovering the real you. This may happen to you many times in your life of soul-discovering, and when it does, the best solution is to share. Remember, even if it is not about what you are feeling, when you talk generally, slowly the fog will clear.

We call this sharing of our truth, the "outflow" which can help us in many ways (e.g., to lose weight, dissolve headaches, diminish nervousness and other ailments associated with spiritual constipation). We can liken it to eating. We process the food and then expel it. If it is nutritious food, it will be converted into all types of body essentials. Spiritual inflow for growth is like that too. We embrace it. It then travels various pathways, enriching and enhancing our life until finally we regroup it, and then we outflow it to cement its training.

There is a spiritual procedure called Group Work, which involves a group of searchers meeting weekly with a booklet of spiritual course notes and a guideline for running it. This can be organised in communities without needing a spiritual consultant other than to regroup the searcher who wishes to lead the Group. It is very productive because within it we can learn how to share with others without inviting opinion and similarly offer others the same respect. We learn how to share from a feeling perspective. We then can take these examples into our life.

As we have reached this far, we have already covered some challenging metaphysics. Now to open insights to the real you!

Chapter Five: Facts of an Energy Being

*Just as a mirror, which reflects all things, is set in its own
container, so too the rational soul is placed in the fragile
container of the body. In this way, the body is governed in its
earthly life by the soul, and the soul contemplates heavenly
things through faith.*

—Hildegard of Bingen

In this chapter we are going to be talking first about you—the real you,
that is—and where you came from.

You are an energy being. This means you have a supply of energy to
get you up in the morning, to give life to the cells in your body, and to
make you feel enlivened. You need a certain amount of energy to keep you
on planet earth; if your energy gets really low, you can become sick. You
have to have enthusiasm for your life to remain healthy and happy. The
will to live can be influenced by whether you are on your spiritual path.
Energy is more vital to you than money because it means life. The more
you have, the greater your enjoyment of life and the easier it is for you to
live in the moment.

This may be an elevated perspective compared to what you are presently familiar with. There are innumerable realities of energy, and each is specific and defined. For the moment we are focusing on the awakening process. We begin the awakening level at the bottom of a pyramid. It is the foundation, and the rest of the structure is going to rest upon it. Because this step is pivotal to all future growth spiritually it is imperative we make the fundamentals indomitable. Presently, at times you may feel your energy unconquerable and at other times vulnerable. These are the fortunes of an energy being, the mysteries of which we can endeavour to divulge.

Your energy is usually charged when you are indulging your passions, such as sharing your visions, inspirations, and experiences. You can feel empowered in these opportunities. Your energy can be thin when you are being dutiful, tired and drained by conditions or lacklustre situations in your life's environment. If you become emotional, you can lose your day's energy in half an hour. If it is anger you are affected by, it can go in ten minutes. Our energy is only half the wattage of our angels at any time and certainly less than that when we are confused.

Without delving deeper at this beginning stage, we can be aware that some people can drain our energy when they are extremely negative and they have used up their own day's supply. They can attempt to source more energy from someone else, either deliberately or innocently. We can witness this with certain people who crave attention. Others add energy naturally because of their love or zest for life or for their present situation. It is preferable to surround ourselves with positive, energized people to avoid being drained and generate procedures for our energy deployment so we don't drain others. When we are able to identify our energy fortunes in certain locations, we will resolve to avoid people or occasions we know create disharmony in our energy balance. The Cutting Energy Technique #10 (refer to chapter seven) is useful for this feeling of being drained. We can change the words to suit the situation.

If you want to know how this energy that is you is constituted, you must acknowledge it is intelligent energy. It has been from the beginning of time, which is not easy to grasp using your thinking nature. It is necessary to absorb it with your feelings. If it is too difficult to digest, leave it on a mental shelf to come back to later, maybe even much later. Truth is like that—it grows on us or in us, and as it does so, it becomes more palatable and uninhibited till we ourselves deem it essential. It may commence its journey though as someone else's idea.

As energy, you can travel at the speed of light. But when you have a body, you may feel more limited (this is, of course, an illusion, but until we stop believing it, we will live the restrictions). Consequently, you may believe it is difficult to drive your body at two kilometres an hour, let alone at the speed of light. Presently we are not talking about your body at all but rather your soul part—the feeling part of you. Even with a body, it is free to travel. It stretches. You may wonder where on earth you are when this happens. You are usually asleep, but you don't have to be. It is one of the perks of freedom you gain from investing in your inner truth. You can consciously learn to travel to wherever you want whenever you want effortlessly.

If we are living life disconnected from our soul part, it is normal to feel that limitation before unfolding our inner truth. It is what having an intellect is all about. Our whole challenge in life is to overcome outside influences and regain our spiritual energy. As we make more soul discoveries, we initiate breakthroughs, which can help reshape our life and make our energy more directed and abundant. Friction, although it feels uncomfortable, helps us to grow spiritually. There is conflict between our intellect and our feelings. We are drawn to heal this disparity between our two natures and close the gap. Usually each time we meet resistance we have some sort of illumination. Bumps on these roadways can help accelerate our spiritual growth.

Whenever there is separation from our inner truth, we can do a technique. This helps stimulate our soul into action and make it grow more conscious and able to access the wisdom we are each endowed with. We can't be a couch potato spiritually and expect our light to expand. As we gather enlightenment, we can experiment with it and action our results. We can do the following technique at any time to assess where we are up to on our pathways to soul-discovery. It can help us to retrieve our true soul perspective.

Technique #6: "Healing the Past"

o   Clear your aura using Technique #7 (located further in this chapter).
o   Read the following technique and memorize it.
o   Close your eyes and take a moment with your guidance and thank them for their backing throughout your life.

o   Ask them to back you for the journey of healing you are about
    to make.
o   Travel with them back to at least twelve months ago. You can
    choose December of the previous year (or any month that is
    twelve months ago) and see any memories you can heal with
    the love you feel right now.
o   Heal those observations gently with your love. Forgive yourself
    for any self-judgments that stimulated emotional feelings.
    Forgive anyone else you may have had similar emotion toward.
    Spread your love over them now to heal this relationship.
o   Now travel over the month of November of the previous year
    (or eleven months ago) and observe any memories lingering
    there needing healing and heal them by forgiving yourself and
    others for any feelings of separation they may have created.
o   Now travel over the months of October and September of the
    previous year (or nine or ten months ago) and do the same.
    Then for the months of August and July of the previous year
    (or seven and eight months ago) and heal whatever is there that
    you sense needs healing.
o   And then do likewise for the months of June and May of the
    previous year (or five and six months ago).
o   Now work the same way with the months of April and March
    of the previous year (or three and four months ago).
o   And now travel back to the months of February and January
    of the previous year (or one and two months ago) and see those
    experiences filled with healing.
o   Now travel forward over all the months of the year to the
    present time and put love over all your memories, sharing
    them as wisdom with your guidance, and thank them for their
    backing during this year.
o   When you feel complete, open your eyes and ask yourself,
    "How do I feel?" Do you feel more connected? Do this
    regularly, even substituting the months for years, then as you
    progress in its efficiency you can substitute it for lifetimes.
o   You can also do it for a month or a week.

Karma

There is a good reason we have a body to slow us down. We need to remember we are immortal—at least our feeling nature is, but when we come here to this planet, we have time slowed down. This is necessary for us to observe tendencies that worked against us in the past, creating flaws in our energy and rectifying them. Habitually people call this karma, but for reasons we will explain later, we are personally driven to correct them because they actually affect us adversely, making us vibrate at a lower frequency in the universe, and this can be quite frustrating. We can metaphorically speaking, call it having a monkey on our back because it slows down our speed of movement.

Our pathways on planet Earth are initially all about fixing stuff— clearing out old negative experiences or memories that cloud or inhibit our opportunity to live a more enlivened and energetic life. Karma is always going to relate to energy improvement because this is what we are here for.

> A man who has not passed through the inferno of his
> passions has never overcome them.
>
> —Carl Jung

To make it easier to understand, consider deeds we have done over lifetimes that have been detrimental to the pure expression of our love primarily for ourselves and subsequently because of that, we were unable to love others. We may have lived a fearful existence, emotional and distracted from the inner beauty we were. We may have reacted rebelliously to challenges. Suppose further that living each of these incidents of estrangement from who we really are can foster a crease in our energy. Our energy is our vehicle we use to travel the universe; you may be able to visualize creases having a distinctive effect on our aeronautics.

To understand this better using a metaphor, we can picture if we were travelling by car we could compare it to a dent. Each time we live our misunderstandings and involve others in them, we can exacerbate our problems. How good would our car travel with dents all over it? After a while, these indentations may start touching wheels or engines and interfering with their performance. Historically we come down here (to planet Earth) to iron out the creases in our energy vehicle, remembering that is all we are and all we have, thereby rendering its enhancement a paramount priority. All we have to do is gain self-awareness to do this and discern the steps we need to take as and when they become necessary. This is a more expanded perspective of karma.

Why, if there are better places to be, do we want to hang out here on planet Earth crippled by a decrease in energy abundance, our wings clipped by the addition of an intellect? You may think you are having a good time here, but are you really? Is life so extraordinary and magnificent that if you had an offer to go elsewhere that embodied all that you could ever dream of, you would pass it up because what you have already is unsurpassable? Delivering ourselves to the reality of our path and purpose creates a great acceleration in the refining of our energy and the achievement of our real goals. By investing in our self-determination, we can change the status quo.

> Man is free at the moment he wishes to be.
>
> —Voltaire

Consider the reality of being energy that is boundless, limitless, omnipotent, all knowing, all-powerful, magnanimous and including many other profound qualities and the only obstacle standing between us and living this potential is a faulty memory. Presently we are endeavouring to assist healing and supporting these recollections we have suppressed, and of course there are opportunistic forces opposed to our education in this regard. We can't really be taught any new illuminations because we already possess all truths we are about to re-learn, and because we are all of those qualities referred to, all we can do is attempt to remind us of what we have concealed from ourselves.

You may want to check with the echo in your feelings technique on that one—I am pretty confident of the response you are going to obtain, and then you can begin revealing some memories for yourself. To help you on your journey, we can do a bit of clearing.

As an energy being, you have an aura, which is your invisible nature. If you were to protect this aura with your life—observe its reaction to your emotions and dismiss what makes it contract or feel pressure, obey its heightened experiences for your direction in life—you will rapidly reach a euphoric state. There are numerous references to this already mentioned through gut feelings and discernment if you cannot visually see or hear the fortunes of your aura.

We are working with the assumption you have creases in your aura because you are here on planet Earth. In your aura are all the deeds you have performed and the people who you have been. Your memories are there. You simply have to find out how to unlock them by stimulating your desire for self-understanding. To further determine the purpose of clearing in life, we can proceed to become all steamed up over absolutely nothing, which appears to be all that matters at the time. We call these emotions, as we have talked about before, and they can block up past memories as well as the memories of the typical behaviour of an energy being. This means we commence to behave like an alien to both planet Earth and the universe when we are overrun by emotion.

These places are really one and the same; one being the small picture of our energy like our intellect, which comes from planet Earth, and the other the big picture of the universe, like our soul part, which comes from the universe. Emotions engender bewilderment blocking our discernment, comparable to when the windscreen on our car becomes fogged up and we can't see where we are going. When we clear it, we relax, and then our energy can do its job and push outward. It protects us from confused entities that influence us to behave in an out of character emotional manner.

> No man is or can be purely individual. The mass of men have only the tiniest touch of individuality: If any. The mass of men live and move, think and feel collectively, and have practically no individual emotions, feelings or thoughts at all.
>
> —D. H. Lawrence

Pride

Using another metaphor, suppose you are a witness to some type of public brawl. Having said that, I certainly hope it never happens to you. We can have emotional, irrational people fighting over an imagined insult. They may believe another person or people are "hurting their pride." We have to ask ourselves, what is pride? It is not a feeling and certainly not a virtue. We know it as one of the seven deadly sins. We can say it is an imagined state of mind, because it does not fit with our true nature.

Because it is fictional how can it be hurt? Unless we want to give power to confusion, which argues in our thoughts, using pride as a weapon against us. Pride is like a very confused misinterpretation of our truth we inherit from generation to generation, which has been continuing for as long as recorded history.

If we were to examine situations where people are irrational, what is it we do? Decide to intervene to reason with them saying, they are acting out of character and it's time they stopped? Right at that moment this may not be a good idea because they might think that you are interfering and contributing to offend their pride and embroil you in their conflict. They have in all likelihood lost their sense of reason and are overcome with emotion. You are no longer talking to what we know as a reasonable person but an illogical one. They are possessed by confused souls who are using them to express their emotions as well. A popular metaphysical term for this is "spooked." At this moment, they are in all probability going to act in ways they will regret later when they are relaxed again and their sense of reason, which comes from their feeling nature, returns.

> The triumph of reason is that it enables us to get along
> with those who do not possess it.
>
> —Voltaire

Although this type of challenge effectively does not confront us in our daily life, we may encounter situations where we become a little emotional. It may well spring from the thought of protecting our pride. It will definitely not come from a feeling of humility. The clearing technique helps us to relax, therefore avoiding these circumstances in the first place, or to heal those existing ups and downs before they become exaggerated.

> Oh! Why should the spirit of mortal be proud? Like a swift-
> fleeting meteor, a fast flying cloud, a flash of lightning, a
> break of the wave, Man passes from life to his rest in the
> grave.
>
> —William Knox

We can liken pride to a dirty old piece of used material we pick up, dust off, and make our own to use, like a neck scarf we wear, to render a glorious life difficult, and then we can fit in with everyone else doing this. It can make a beautiful, special person totally inflicted and afflicted by it like a virus. Working with pride equals regression on our spiritual pathways to freedom.

Pride has its own ego. This is where the majority of our conceptual problems which contribute to mood swings emanate from. Suppose we could control our ego to simply give us the impetus to extend our stay on planet Earth for soul-discovery and to expand our humility; it would be transformational. Taming our pride and its concepts with our humility pays the greatest spiritual dividends, and if we could encourage everyone to invest in humility, we might have a planet of wise, detached, generous, compassionate, caring, and loving human beings.

> Confusion is a word we have invented for an order which is not understood.
>
> —Henry Miller

Certain mood swings can really be an enemy of ours. Because there are numerous people who don't have control of their emotions doesn't mean it is a mode of behaviour we want to accept from ourselves or from others. Bizarre as it may seem this behaviour is now commonplace among the populace. This is because we have become conditioned to living in our heads. There is a whole profession that has evolved in analysing it, as a normal part of life and devoted to studying it. We can therefore boldly say our out-of-balance conduct has now become so obvious it is regarded as normal.

> What the weak head with strongest bias rules, is pride, the never-failing vice of fools.
>
> —Alexander Pope

To avoid emotion, we need to develop and use our discernment in life to work out why we are being affected emotionally and take time out to heal any such interference in energy first, long before we become emotional. Discernment is a big subject and deserves a more extensive application.

An effective tool to dissolve pride and stimulate the power of humility is an affirmation we can repeat numerous times in situations where our pride is manipulating or modifying our potential success. 'I am nothing, I am no one, I am just love.' When we say this confused souls can't influence us to work against our better interests.

Discernment

Our aura is part of the energy identity we have. One of our energy centres we are going to be talking about later is dedicated to the task of receiving messages. Because we are energy, we have messages hitting us from not just all over the world but all over the universe as well. Our energy is tuned in, even if our intellect is not. Like watching the news, we have our own channel that receives news reports twenty-four hours per day. We may watch some of it as it relates to us, but mostly it doesn't. Our energy centre is like a giant satellite that delivers these messages to our feelings, and we can stop and ask our discernment for a breakdown on concerns that can linger and make their way through our filters.

The best way to identify this is when we have a feeling of being apprehensive about circumstances in our life and do not know why. We can, once we use our inner truth more successfully, stop and process a "what, when, where, and why" of this disquiet, and then we can choose to remove it from our reality. If we have a busy head or are in the grip of aroused reactions, it may mean our discernment of the messages we are receiving is roaming without a signal or is switched off. We can further inflame our lack of discernment by analysing the concern as maybe having a bad day and accept it without any real explanation. There are better ways, as you might conclude, of living our life. Discernment is one of those refinements that spiritual investments provide us with in time.

> The firmness with which the people have withstood the late abuses of the press, the discernment they have manifested between truth and falsehood, show that they may safely be trusted to hear everything true and false, and to form a correct judgment.
>
> —Thomas Jefferson

Technique #7: Clearing Technique

This technique will help you keep your energy compact at all times.

1. Stand and relax and take a deep breath in through your nose and out through your mouth.
2. With the fingertips of your right hand, gently rub the centre of your forehead (third eye), fingers hardly touching it, until you feel relaxed.
3. Leaving your right hand on your third eye, bring the fingertips of your left hand up to your third eye, meeting your right hand.
4. Gently draw both hands over your brow, right hand on right side and left hand on left side, and move them over your temple, going down both sides of your jaw.
5. Strongly shake your hands once in front of you to recharge them. Your wrists need to be held limp.
6. Take both hands simultaneously to your third eye again. With your fingertips of both hands touching, move both hands over the back of your head and then bring them around the back of your neck and around and under your chin till they meet in front of you.
7. Strongly shake your hands once again to recharge them.
8. Repeat steps three through seven until you feel chills, a warm inner glow, or more relaxed.
9. As you do this technique, say an affirmation, such as, "From the love within me, I clear and cleanse my body and re-energize my soul" or whatever words you feel positive about, like, "from the God within I clear and cleanse my body and re-energize my soul."

   a. When gently rubbing your third eye, you say, "From the love within me" or whatever affirmation you choose.
   b. When bringing your hands down the side of your temples and jaw, you say, "I clear and cleanse my body."
   c. When taking your hands over your head and the back of your neck, you say, "And I re-energize my soul."

This Clearing Technique can be done mentally by asking for backing from your angels to clear your aura and picturing in your mind's eye your hands doing the movement while saying the affirmation to yourself at the same time. If you are in public or in the presence of other people, it is a better solution to do it discretely to avoid "cranking people up." It is more powerful to do the physical movements initially, particularly till it becomes automated. It is best to use this technique to precede all techniques that you undertake. It will enhance your energy to be more lucid and fluent in its execution.

Grief

You may believe grief, for instance, is an emotion, but strangely, it more often is a natural feeling—we do grieve over people, situations, losses, character judgments, relationships, and many other involvements. It is okay and natural to do that, and when it is finalized, we are done. If it is prolonged and we start making it part of our life mission, then it essentially has become intellectual grief.

If grieving is a process necessary for us to regain our feeling of involvement again for our energy, in the absence of a special person in our life who has departed in their physical form, a lost opportunity, or the departure of a confused loved one in our aura, it is natural. If it is a protracted preoccupation we involve ourselves in because we have lost our feeling for living and start yearning for the old life shared with those departed to return, it has become unnatural.

One idea comes from our thinking nature, and one is a sense of releasing from our feeling nature. When we do feel this yearning for someone who has passed on, which may last for years, often it can be because the person has not made transition, as we have already talked about. Living in the past is a very spiritually damaging preoccupation because we are feeding an illusion and are stagnating. It is comparable to eating mouldy food. We have to live in the present, or we will know no joy in life. Living in the future makes us wither spiritually because we are living delusions about our life. We can perhaps relate it to the following:

> We remember yesterday, but can't live there;
> We plan for tomorrow, but don't build there . . .

Therefore our philosophy for life can perhaps be:

> We live in the moment to sow seeds for tomorrow's harvest, building upon our past success and avoiding the repetition of our failures.
>
> Finish each day and be done with it you have done what you could. Some blunders and absurdities no doubt crept in; forget them as soon as you can. Tomorrow is a new day; begin it well and serenely and with too high a spirit to be encumbered with your old nonsense.
> —Ralph Waldo Emerson

Even worse is the possibility these loved ones may be in our aura, attempting to live the old life, which is a toxic situation for both of us. We may be holding them there with our yearning, or their refusal to leave our aura may make us pine for them, and they are then unable to move on to a greater consciousness because of it. We both become trapped in a time warp, living in the past, neither progressing as situations around us deteriorate because we can no longer manage our life with passion and involvement.

The best alternative to yearning is to accept and allow the fate of our loss its natural progression. Don't fight our grief but instead, follow it, trusting there is a purpose to it, presently undefined. We can love the person who has passed on unconditionally, which will help us to make the right decisions to back their transition without selfishly holding onto them because of our refusal to accept their passing and/or to meet the challenges their loss represents. Our attitude will support their quest to find their own pathways, doing what they have to do. If we nurse regret for lost opportunities, we need to learn to trust the refinement we have garnered through these situations to ensure we do not repeat our mistakes.

> Nothing happens to anybody, which he is not fitted by nature to bear.
> —Marcus Aurelius

Although it may be difficult to digest at the moment, the more we can detach from outcomes, the more love we will have to share with more people.

Our Two Natures in Review

As our two natures can be fairly confusing; it may be necessary to recap on them. Our thinking nature is our intellect. It comes with our body, and we (and our situation) train it in our first seven years. It is as a result of this training that we pick up emotional habit patterns and play them like they are a part of our script for living. Initially we do sustain these patterns to heal them, but after a qualifying time, they can be written out of our life script as we move toward more self-understanding and control of our emotions.

> The intellectual attainments of a man who thinks for himself resemble a fine painting, where the light and shade are correct, the tone sustained, the colour perfectly harmonized; it is true to life. On the other hand, the intellectual attainments of the mere man of learning are like a large palette, full of all sorts of colours, which at most are systematically arranged, but devoid of harmony, connection and meaning.
> —Arthur Schopenhauer

We can say our intellect typically picks up its own story, which has often little to do with our real life. Because of these emotional habit patterns (or concepts) we have collected, we can believe we are going to perish, fear abandonment, live rejection, feel impoverished, be afraid of the future, make people authority figures, own depression, and many similarly confused ideas about ourselves or life, whereas none of this is part of our real purpose and can with awareness be circumnavigated.

We have to exercise control over our thoughts. They do not spring zealously up from our feelings with purity and respect for who we are. They are more manufactured, and as such they are open to contamination from the ideas of others or our conditioning. Accordingly, we have to safeguard our thoughts and discipline them to avoid exposure to negativity, distracting influences, or programming. These misinterpretations constipate our sensitivity. We need to heal their debilitating patterns. By now they may have furnished us with bad habits that can lock us in vacillating thought processes. By controlling our thoughts, we can begin our return to peace within, our natural state of being. To simplify it, all we have to do is watch our thoughts, although in practice, habits can prove tenacious to shift.

> It's a rough road that leads to the heights of greatness.
>
> —Seneca

Why? Because any predisposition to conduct ourselves with limitations is best coaxed out of us. We otherwise keep going back to that automated mode of conduct that is familiar and may not even recognise these idiosyncrasies. Alternatively we can criticize ourselves for not being perfect, and this locks us tighter in the clutches of the habit, thus harnessing us to a sense of hopelessness. Another inhibiting quality that can stagnate our spiritual growth is when we want to be positive and become addicted to the good news about ourselves and reject the truth for what it really is, which can help us fall into the category of living delusion.

> Each player must accept the cards life deals him or her: but once they are in hand, he or she alone must decide how to play the cards in order to win the game.
>
> —Voltaire

Our I.D.

It is critical to listen in to yourself and your thoughts and try to identify which ones carry concepts that are not healthy for you. This is called your inner dialogue, where all the battles for your energy are won or lost. When you observe the people around you at any given moment, what you are witnessing is the outcome of their inner dialogue aptly termed their 'I.D.' It can make us young or old before our time, tired, drained, or enthusiastic and energized. It can make us happy or sad, joyful or depressed, rich or poor, healthy or unhealthy. It has little to do with physical outside influences.

Our inner dialogue asserts endless control over us. Consequently, if we think it is part of us and believe its environmental training does not detrimentally influence us, we become its captive. When you hear people saying, "I want freedom" or "I am finally free" in metaphysical terms, this is often what they are talking about. They are talking about being locked in their body by their misunderstandings or feeling free when they realize and heal limiting concepts and their energy is liberated, thus moving to greater heights. To conquer our thoughts, we have to keep them in check and make them work for us. This is to use awareness and self-discipline. There is a technique you can do that can help you stimulate awareness.

Technique #8: How to Read Energy

o Visualize a person in front of you, preferably someone you don't know well. Maybe it's someone you saw in your surroundings or on television.

o Close your eyes and picture the person in front of you.

o What is it you are feeling? Create a blank mind and an empty screen. Now what do you feel?

o Do you feel anxious? Frustrated? Relaxed? Calm? Peaceful? Undecided? Or other emotions not mentioned?

o Keep a notepad handy, and write your emotions down. It is possible these are your feelings or emotions, or you may be sensing the feelings or emotions of the person you are reading. It involves practice. This is what you do at the speed of light anyway. It is possible that you may have forgotten to discern as a moment-by-moment reality. This is part of the amnesia we have been talking about.

o Do this with people you hardly know first till you feel more confident. Then experiment with people in your more immediate environment with their permission. If you know them well or there is someone who you know is working on the same thing you are, self—discovery, choose him or her and then allow him or her to read you. Ask the other person to share how factual your reading was and share honestly with him or her also. Repeat it if necessary.

This is a good exercise to practice your sensitivity. Often people do not know what they are feeling and the information you share may be confronting for them, but it is usually very healing for both parties. Because it is the opposite of being nice or being polite, we may feel reprimanded by others' opinions of us. It is normal for us to feel this as our exploration for inner truth begins. Our feelings can't be hurt. Remember, we are the ocean. Therefore, a little courage can support us to elevate ourselves from the masses. But always be aware the truth is unpopular with most people initially. Therefore, our efforts to always protect our energy must be significant. Many warriors of the truth have been persecuted in our history; being aware of this can help you understand people will defend their pride at any cost. Be sensitive about what to share and what is not to divulge.

Make it light, fun, and always positive. Our angels are charismatic in the manner of their sharing. Remember, regardless of how confident you believe a person to be, they will perhaps have doubts about themselves. We never want to feed the confusion around others, hence positive input can truly help to dismantle these doubts and make our experiments in soul-discovery a profound learning and investment opportunity.

> To be yourself in a world that is constantly trying to make
> you something else is the greatest accomplishment.
> —Ralph Waldo Emerson

Awareness—Opening Our Sensitivity

We gain awareness through our sensitivity, which is the intellect of our soul. Now we are expanding our vocabulary to incorporate two intellects, one that came with our body and one that comes with our soul. As we evolve, we appreciate the importance of what we are sensing. It is how we work with awareness, placing our life under a microscope of discernment and using our inner truth to discover meaning. On an energy level, there are copious opportunities in each moment for us to learn about our background, and as this book will not have the scope to deal with it, we are only going to target the necessities. These will be facts you have to acquaint yourself with.

There are initially numerous energies for us to identify, but perhaps the most notable of all (apart from our own) present in and around us is that of souls without bodies. They are souls like you and me who have passed on (relinquished their body) and are confused about where to go and what to do. They often hang around us. Each of us seems to lure our share of these souls, and they interfere with our happiness. They have found a way through our bad habits (inhibiting thoughts and subsequent emotions) to penetrate our energy. It sounds like those alien movies you may have watched or even vampire ones—and yes it is true, the inspiration for most of these movies comes from the real-life drama of us fighting for our own

74

energy on a daily basis from confused souls who want to drain us because they don't have any energy of their own or very low energy.

> A sensible man will remember that the eyes may be confused in two ways—by a change from light to darkness or from darkness to light; and he will recognize the same thing happens to the soul.
>
> —Plato

Remember we talked about our life being reflective. There are many movies that mirror our spiritual struggles with ourselves that are helpful until we can consciously identify them in our life. If we sometimes feel overwhelmed by the negativity around us and despondent, believing we have to fix the world, the good news is we can now relax because we know all we have to improve is our own inner dialogue and the world around us changes miraculously as do the people in it we may be having difficulty with. This energy is such a powerful force that it can enhance or deteriorate our surroundings moment by moment.

I have observed how the price of real estate in the locality has risen when only one person elevates their consciousness well beyond the bounds of others in the area. I have seen the lights of a city extinguished with no known cause by a person hitting "a peak of energy" from doing a group of courses and clearing souls around them. I have had to instruct people to pull their aura in when they are in a "heightened state" and venture out to mingle with the public, causing waiters to drop consecutive trays around them and other people incessantly talking like they were administered a drug. Searchers can be wreaking havoc through their inexperience of an expanded aura. As we refine our energy, it can become a weapon we have to learn to use or it will break machines, burst light bulbs, and affect others. This is a testament to the realization of energy changes. I have people phone me regularly complaining about equipment breaking down and its replacement suffering the same fate until they have lessons in aura management. The benefits of a heightened state far outweigh these inconveniences.

How wonderful would it be if everyone knew that the only real problem they can have in their life is with themselves, and when they resolve it within, their unlimited natures can finally present themselves and their personality problems fade into oblivion? Their true love nature emerges from within and dilutes the power of adversity.

> Art is a microscope which the artist fixes on the secrets of his soul, and shows to people these secrets which are common to all.
>
> —Leo Tolstoy

There are many categories of confused souls around us, but for the purposes of not wanting to overwhelm perhaps an already stretched friendship that is between you and the revelations in the book, we can simplify them at this stage into two categories: the negative dark (confused souls) or the positive light (our angels or angels of the light) and only open wider revelations gradually.

It would be prudent to acknowledge the advancement of our metaphysics already. The truth is a very powerful and potent adversary of confusion that ravages our life, stealing our happiness, captivating us in trivial pursuits, and rendering our omnipotence impotent.

> Sometimes in our confusion, we see not the world as it is, but the world through eyes blurred by the mind.
>
> —Anonymous

Chapter Six: Confused Souls

Everything is fine today that is our illusion.

—Voltaire

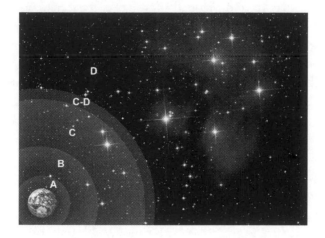

The negative energy we are now referring to is a whole narrative of its own. Confused souls, as we have made countless references to, are those people who did not accomplish what they came to planet Earth to achieve, namely their purpose, and therefore left unfulfilled. This could sound like many people we know. When they did depart, they were yearning to be back on planet Earth, and they deliberately or inadvertently ignored their angels and the whole process of transition to obsessively attempt to pursue their old life. Without a body, it became very difficult to accomplish that. If you saw the movie *The Sixth Sense*, it was almost an entirely accurate description of what happens to us when we pass on with misunderstandings. It is a good idea to review these movies when with new awareness you can have the fulfilment of recognition. There are many other movies that demonstrate some fundamental spiritual truths for us to witness. As you observe in these movies, most of these souls are not intentionally disruptive but confused about where they need to be. The movie *The Lovely Bones* depicted the journey of a loved one. If you have not seen it, I highly recommend it.

To assist us to grasp how a person can become a confused soul, let us surmise for a moment that we become one. (Not that we can be right now because we still have a body and this makes us connected to the energy source, the system of Spirit, angels guiding us, and an opportunity, a lifetime.) Let us imagine the following scenario.

Some time ago we came to planet Earth, and we didn't work on our creases (or correctly termed flaws). Essentially, though, it is metaphorically speaking. We may have developed more creases because we wasted our time, and our energy became limp and unenlightened. When we passed on, we may have been full of regrets about our life, lamenting what we had not done or we may have been thinking about loved ones we left behind (still living our maze) and generally be feeling unfulfilled or feeling exploited by our choices and perhaps even harbouring a grudge. Our feelings if unawakened, kept replaying the memory of planet Earth repeatedly, and we were looking down at our loved ones in a possessive or obsessive way and wanting to continue living our old life. We became dazed and bewildered about passing on.

When we do this, we are avoiding making transition, looking down at the past stagnating instead of up toward the future and moving with our angels, who are there to guide us at this time. We begin to become trapped, living neither one system nor the other. We no longer have our normal source of energy coming from our angels to move us around because we are not adhering to ours' and theirs' system of evolution, but instead, we resist it.

We then become earthbound, very short on power, impelling us to hang around people we knew and use their energy (power) without procuring their permission. This can happen because they are unaware we are doing it, or if they are conscious, they may be ignorant of the consequences. Usually they are familiar with the feel of our energy. Therefore they open their aura to permit us entry. They let down their guard.

In order to stay around these people, we have to keep them talking about our last memories of what happened to us on planet Earth. They believe they are thinking about us and may suppose they are yearning for us. These misunderstandings can anchor us to their energy, and we can embark on a plan to share their life with them. We may want to share our time with other members of our family (if they are available) as we did when we were in a physical body. An easy way to understand it is to realize we can without a body travel anywhere we want, whereas with a body we become limited.

As a confused soul, there is little else we dwell on other than the memory of this last lifetime. We usually, depending on our state of consciousness, do not remember we are eternal and believe we are still living our old life and that is all there is. We can then be manipulated by other souls who know the ropes and can use us to their advantage. We have sources of energy we have access to that they can steal from us, without us even being aware of this process. Because they are more refined they can move above us whilst we concentrate our attention below.

Moving on in Time

As the pages of our book of life turn and the people we knew as loved ones pass on, we become less and less energized in our confused state without the energy of our loved ones to rely on. There is always the possibility if they grow spiritually in their lifetime and become more enlightened, we may benefit inclusively from their advancement because we are residing around them. If we still remain unconscious, we can then drift around for years searching for others to talk to about our misunderstandings, until our loved ones reincarnate.

> And when life's sweet fable ends,
> Soul and body part like friends;
> No quarrels, murmurs, no delay;
> A kiss, a sigh and so away.

> —Richard Crashaw

It is not a very nice place to be, and this is why it is referred to as hell. We are in a type of torment all the time because we have no inner peace and are ignorant of how to find it. There is no fulfilment, contentment, joy, or happiness in our life. It is essential for those who know they have loved ones in their aura that they endeavour to help them discover the procedure to follow necessary for their transition. Many people can inadvertently keep a selfish dialogue because of inexperience, and then, when in turn they pass on as their loved ones did before them and perhaps reincarnate again, they don't even remember these once-treasured souls from their last lifetimes.

These souls are now abandoned, waiting for their family to reincarnate. When they find them again, they can be frustrated because their family members (now in a new lifetime) do not remember them. They are then experienced as confused thoughts and emotions. It is not a positive outcome for either party.

Depending on the level of our attainment as a confused soul, we will hang with people who think the same as we do, including other souls who have passed on like us, and we can actually congregate together looking for people to engage (and draining their energy at the same time). It is not much of an existence, considering the other prospects we have before us.

Anyone who converses with us when we are confused this way will lose energy and may not care too much about it because in all probability they don't realize how important the energy they are losing is to them.

> When an unclean spirit is gone out of a man, he walketh
> through dry places, seeking rest; and finding none, saith,
> I will return unto my house whence I came out.
> —Luke 11:24

There was a time I did a tour offering people opportunity to connect their departed loved ones. Many of the people I met knew they had loved ones in their aura and refused to release them. I was less experienced with this mischievous energy at the time and anguished over these souls trapped through the deliberate mishandling of their living loved ones. After they left me all they felt was satisfaction with the confirmation. Many attracted to the service were part of spiritual churches and amateurish in their beliefs about this process. Despite appealing to their love nature to be compassionate, they refused to allow their loved ones peace. I then directed the reading they paid for directly to the soul who was caught. If they wanted to leave I gave them passage. The souls who have thanked me have been numerous and my cup felt filled.

No wonder the scriptwriters, producers, and directors of movies about this, including the actors who accept the roles, feel the impetus to produce these amazing movies that educate us about our life hereafter. They help us reclaim the truth about ourselves while they follow their individual inspirations, and we all benefit from the healing. The lyrics of songs can help educate us similarly.

These I believe, are people on planet Earth very connected and living their opportunities as scribes for Spirit in this way. How often does a movie or song suddenly appear adding a message of meaning to our life at the most appropriate time? The whole format of movies duplicates the system of downloads of information we receive from our angels, each day offering a new sequel with the people in our life playing characters in our script, usually without our conscious contributions. We are simultaneously playing out characters in their script, which is often why certain people fall out of favour with each other at particular times. They are generally appropriately healing past lives. I have witnessed this hundreds of times. We need to relax with the process and keep inflowing love and outflowing forgiveness or change the order of these words, whichever works (see Technique #17 in chapter ten).

Hell Revisited

> We are each our own devil, and we make this world our hell.
>
> —Oscar Wilde

Hell, as we have referred to countless times, we can call an unawakened state where we are influenced by whatever mood is in our surroundings. Because we have not been discriminating in our energy awareness of people and situations, we can be easily manipulated. If we were not awakened at all when we passed on, we can become caught floating around planet Earth, unable to really attach to any opportunities. We are perhaps angry our life is not the same as it was and frustrated and anxious that our challenges within it are becoming more difficult.

Many unawakened people can live a very disquieting existence consisting of ups and downs that feel like they are in hell much of the time. This is because we are electromagnetic energy. Like attracts like. When we feel anxious or frustrated, souls who are feeling like that become anchored to our energy. They vibrate at the same frequency we do at that moment. They float around us, agreeing with the thoughts we are having and magnifying the situation because our whole emotional misunderstanding can become amplified by their presence.

Confused souls are never happy because they don't have energy. When they get energy (our energy), they feel better, hence their main drive for their subsistence is to engage us in their conversation. It makes them feel better, which we will feel as inhibiting thoughts. As we shrink they expand. As a consequence, of course, they will stay around us for as long as we allow them to. When we calm down and relax, our energy vibration changes and becomes more like concrete to them or a brick wall, and they have to move out.

> Life is thickly sown with thorns and I know no other remedy than to pass quickly through them. The longer we dwell on our misfortunes, the greater is their power to harm us.
>
> —Voltaire

Purgatory

Purgatory is a state of mind or aptly termed an intellectual jungle. When people have many intellectual theories about life they become fixated about and don't entertain a bigger picture of being a soul on planet Earth learning and growing, it is possible when they pass on, they will go into a zone called purgatory. They remain there until they clarify this misinterpretation of their truth or are healed by learning through the insights and spiritual growth of those loved ones or colleagues who they hang around. When you say affirmations you can help heal these souls.

It is this level of confusion that souls with too much dogma, bigotry racism, and out-of-balance theology inhabit. The souls here are very inflexible in their ideas about life. They can squabble for their point of view and preach to anyone who will listen to them about their beliefs and theories on life. They have the tendency to always think they are right in these assessments, taking as much of our time as we are willing to part with to similarly indoctrinate us. They can believe they have the answers for everyone else as well. In fact, it is perhaps much the same as they did on planet earth.

I am sure you know people like this; it is very difficult to have a conversation navigating our way around subjects they have a strong belief system about. When they pass on, they can be caught in believing their way is the only way or is the right way, or their religion, politics or obsession is the only one to follow. It is very difficult for these souls to elevate themselves. They can have strong points of view on many subjects, including the right way to live, eat, parent, or whatever else they may feel strongly about, and when they are around us, we will hear these types of thoughts or preconceptions, which can be powerful condemnations of others. In summarizing its potential influence on us, if we are strong in theories, it may be beneficial for us to reflect on changing our perspectives to listen to other people's truths respectfully, because this is a very argumentative and bullying type of energy we do not want to attract in our life.

This is mostly referred to as purgatory. It makes it easier for us to define it if we put familiar names to these out-of-balance states of consciousness. Of course, there are varying levels to each of these zones. We can even define these levels to in-balance and out-of-balance. There have been a few movies echoing this state of consciousness.

> Prejudices are what fools use for reason.
>
> —Voltaire

Limbo

The next level of confusion we are delving into is often referred to as *limbo*. This zone involves souls who knew about growing spiritually and its value but did not get around to it. They were too busy indulging in their life's maze to find the opportunity to evolve spiritually, delaying their participation in their life mission until it was too late. They were perhaps too comfortable earning money or following a career or sport obsessively without finding balance for their thoughts and feelings to invest in. They are often referred to as fence sitters.

When they pass on, they go to limbo, where other souls were equally living as spectators instead of participants. Spiritually they prefer social trivia to self-discovery. They indulge in concepts of prestige or competition, being stuck in their ways or pursuing a career in earning money and collecting material possessions in a confused way. This zone is all about comfort (e.g., collecting white goods obsessively to make life more agreeable and less challenged).

These souls can predominantly live an overly cautious attitude toward their physical welfare preferring not to personally participate in any challenging sports. They can encourage us to be a couch potato. They love TV. When we snow or water ski, horse ride, sky jump or any of these active sports we lose many of these souls. They literally fall out of our aura.

In limbo these souls can still be waiting for the big opportunity to come to them, languishing there while they waste time daydreaming because they don't realize they are the master designers of their own destiny. Until they become contributors to their spiritual evolution themselves, nothing is going to happen.

> While we are postponing, life speeds by.
>
> —Seneca

These souls can make sitting still and doing nothing feel normal and attractive, even sometimes a form of art and alternatively moving out of comfort zones changing offices, houses, employment, cities, countries or travelling to new destinations full of trepidation. When they are more enlightened, they can meet the challenges of progressing more enthusiastically at this level. Advancement is what life on planet Earth is really all about. Meeting and overcoming challenges is how we become passionate about our lives as we test our invincible natures.

> He sat on the fence so long that the iron has entered his soul.
>
> —David Lloyd George

Zones of Confusion: A (Hell), B (Purgatory), C (Limbo)

To summarize, we have been talking about the zones of confusion that circle planet Earth and where souls get trapped when they pass on in an unawakened state. The A-Zone is known as hell. These A-Zone souls are angry, anxious, awkward, frustrated, self-indulgent, and unaware. Or when souls are unbalanced, biased, bigoted, belligerent, or bewildered, they are in what we call B-Zone, additionally known as purgatory. When they are awakened and aware but not committed, living comfort zones and waiting for life to hand them the big opportunities, this is known as C-Zone or limbo. We can identify they have concepts of being cautious, comfortable, competitive, controlling, cunning, and conniving.

This is what negative energy is. It is people who have passed on without bothering to open to soul-discovery and have become caught in a misunderstanding about who they are, where they are going, and what they are avoiding now. And because they made these choices in their life, when they pass on they become trapped in these zones of confusion.

When we do our Clearing Technique #7 (refer to chapter five), we can loosen up the thoughts in our mind, and we can clear our aura of these souls. When we are relaxed, they really can't involve us in their emotional views of life or influence us. They may try to harass us to become involved in their discourse again once we have clarified what is our true energy, but if we stay relaxed, avoiding the concepts of caution, stagnation, competition, and manipulation, we can become our own person more consistently. Again it comes back to our own inner dialogue and how militant we are to keep it uncontaminated. It is a choice we can make in each moment of our life as its adventures and misadventures come calling.

C-D Zone of Limitation

There is another zone not well known by many that is in a train track between C-Zone and D-Zone. Because the energy there is increasingly more cultivated than the level below them, they think they are angels. We call them grey angels. They are neither one thing nor the other. They are in between transition and confusion. Often these souls are very refined and know a great deal about confusion and angels but have not made the final step of letting go of planet Earth. They are often captivated by a loved one, whom they cannot bear to part with. They may feel the person yearning for them, and they may wait in that zone until their loved one passes on also. They can be entrapped by ideas that they have planetary opportunities to finish, particularly if their life was terminated abruptly or earlier than they wanted to leave. These souls can assert a great deal of influence over us.

We can feel "possessed" by them, which is very different from the other zones—where A-Zone souls affect us in our emotions, B-Zone souls in our thoughts, C-Zone souls in our aspirations, C-D Zone souls are more "possession souls" like that departed loved one.

There are movies that depict souls with total possession of a person. Some are extreme cases exploited, which is testament to the unfolding energy awareness of the populace.

There are now tables available to heal these souls quickly and cleanly. These advanced tables are offered to the public in certain parts of the world and involve a specifically trained trance consultant to remove these troublesome souls. In the meantime, the techniques in this book are more than adequate to help us avoid such possession initially. The Cutting Technique #10 (refer chapter seven) and the Clearing Technique #7 (refer chapter five) in particular can help protect us. In circumstances some of the new movies reveal where there is total possession, the host is usually allowing it to happen, therefore complete rejection of participation can will most souls away, although in actuality many of these cases are exaggerated for theatrical purposes.

Our angels can provide protection for us with their aura, releasing it as we ourselves can discern and heal souls. To people I train, as and when they are awakened, I encourage them to take the beginning trance training primarily to heal their own aura in zones A, B, and C and then to offer a service to others (see the section on Tables at the end of this chapter). It then makes it easier to recognize most souls with a cleansed aura and seek the next step to healing them. As I emphasized before, the correct training is essential. I have witnessed many cases of possession when sensitive untrained people believe they are releasing souls for others because they can see them but in fact are taking possession of the souls themselves.

We own our aura, and souls do not have a right to be there. When we understand that, we have to become indignant about this violation of our energy and ask our angels for help to shift them if we are not trained and are unable to find trained trance consultants. This training cannot be reinvented. It is a refined system already on planet Earth, and Spirit does not duplicate its services. That is why coordination with our angels for the integrity of the message being shared is essential.

One of the many healings I performed in this zone was for a grandmother who begged me to help out when her daughter-in-law rapidly changed in personality after her mother died. Her mother had been hospitalized for a mental disorder, and on one of her releases, she covered herself with petrol and burned herself to death in front of her daughter. The daughter, now the mother of a young girl herself, began, shortly after her mother's death, to cut herself with knives and started to act out her mother's disorder, although she had no prior history of this behaviour. (The mother was now in her aura.) On releasing the mother from the daughter's aura, I found it was actually her grandmother who had similarly affected her mother on her death, making it a family tradition of mental illness. After the healing of both women, life resumed to its normality again.

There are many case histories I could reveal, but this book is too basic for such details to be shared. To wrap up, I would like to share in one recent healing a woman I knew nursed her dying mother for several months. The mother was very depressed for several years refusing to leave her house and confined herself to her bed. Eventually she became ill and passed on. The daughter who nursed her was very involved in life and a dynamic individual. After her mother died she became extremely depressed and confined herself to her bed and her family were concerned about this drastic change in her personality. This change persisted till I connected her mother with her angels and the daughter was able to return to her normal life. When we grieve for too long, we eventually forget how joyful life was before we allowed a depressed lost loved one into our aura. We perceive our life through the eyes of our depressed loved one. Many people I have met have held such loved ones close for years, gradually diminishing their enjoyment in life.

Other Souls at D-Level

> If there were no God, it would have been necessary to invent him.
>
> —Voltaire

There are other types of confusion that we are not going to talk about because until we are really discerning in our understanding, we can't relate to them and certainly not at the awakening level. They do influence us substantially, and we can remove them as we grow in enlightenment because we can recognize how they affect us. (Many go as we win back control of our aura.) They cannot be moved effectively until this time when we become aware of them.

I have had extensive experience with all of these souls, particularly in healing them, therefore other books on the subject will follow in time when we are all better acquainted with the subject matter.

Trance Healing Tables

There are separate, distinct and individual Trance Healing Tables available for each of the A, B, C, C-D and D level souls.

The A level involves three people, a control and two healers, equal in training. The A level souls as we have spoken about in length are very unawakened and emotional. The tables are therefore compassionate and educational for the souls, connecting them with their new reality gently and reverently.

The B level souls require a special table, which has very little dialogue and can involve as many trained healers and controls as there are available. The souls are given direction and connected very abruptly with their angels, thus avoiding their dogma or arguments to interfere with the process and providing a swift directed healing.

The C level souls have a similar table to the A level. The souls already aware are enlightened as to their misunderstandings respectfully and with their cooperation are connected with their angels who are present at the healing.

All three tables help the person having a healing to identify with their misunderstandings.

The tables become available in a community when three or more people decide to take the training in all three tables or a specific one or two tables, and offer the public healings to their community.

Anyone can train to do this. The courses are short, no more than a day's training for each of the three levels although the energy of such potential trainees needs to be ready for such investments of cleansing their aura to ensure such a giant leap in consciousness does not overwhelm their aura.

The other levels of souls at C-D and D require more involved training and experience and have been explained in more detail under their respective paragraphs.

Chapter Seven: Our States of Consciousness—Unawakened, Awakening to Soul Awareness, and Internship

Men hate the individual whom they call avaricious only because nothing can be gained from him.

—Voltaire

Awareness of these zones, particularly in their confused states, has already been introduced, but we can now delve a little deeper. They have an in-balance and out-of-balance state. Even though we experience confusion, it can be a very productive part of our healing. As we discover out-of-balance, confused ways and reform them, the souls around us likewise can heal their misunderstandings.

This is a positive outcome for everyone. Because of the intimidating nature of confusion, we are driven to search for answers ensuring we don't fall too far into negativity. We can, in essence, blame confusion for every mishap in our life. The defining moment, though, is reconciling why they are there in the first place. We can confidently assume our state of consciousness needs upgrading.

There are multiple steps to our enlightenment, and this is only a brief explanation. Each of them transforms our state of being, but for the purpose of introducing its cognizance, we present facts more relative to the subject now. To assimilate this, we can visualize ascending the steps of a pyramid. With each enormous leap up, we elevate our view. When we reach the top, we have a very different perspective from our impressions on the first step. This is how expanding our state of consciousness works. We cannot understand anything beyond the realm of our own limited viewpoint at any moment. The windows of the universe open a wider view as we show our loyalty and sincerity and integrity with ourselves and then naturally with others. To clarify this further it is different from the many messages and messengers of a psychic nature given as a service. Our angels do not engage in giving these type of personal readings through the untrained. They come from grey angels, which is why they are often correct about the past but completely inaccurate about the future. Grey angels, like everyone else, can only speculate about what will happen, because they are confused. An educated guess is their best insight.

We have already mentioned the angelic realm. On some level, we may already be aware of this state of being, even if we don't really have any truly formed ideas about it. It is sufficient to know that the further we ascend into the universe through the zones, the more affluent energy we will meet.

If we are prepared, our aura has regained its point, and we will feel a total sense of being, which is elevated the higher we go. As water finds its own level, we find our state of consciousness. If we attempt to transcend beyond our level, it will feel like concrete we can't break through, similar to being in a body unable to move through walls.

The more abundant the energy, the more enhanced the feeling of utopia. If our energy is more sophisticated, we will magnetize cultivated people to fellowship with, and our experience will be more sublime. They will be more respectful and energy wise seeking their higher selves toward more the reflection, as we know God to be.

Rather than imagining this as a physical place, it is better understood as a state of being. This means when you are having good-quality thoughts, they can provoke some very profound and meaningful episodes in your life. You can liken these experiences to a state of being that is awakened and effective in producing good-feeling exposure. It will last for as long as you can keep the quality of thoughts or lack of thoughts constant and you can attain perhaps, even if it is only briefly, a glimpse of heaven or the reality of living in a state of being one with all things.

Simply said, as long as our attitude about our lives and ourselves is constantly positive and solution oriented, confused souls cannot drain our energy. The more energy we have, the happier and more fulfilled we feel, and subsequently, the easier it is to stay directed and focused.

Energy is similar to how we identify money if we don't believe we have enough of it. We can, in these circumstances, consider a certain amount of money would eliminate or negate all life's difficulties. This is, of course, an illusion, and it is rather energy that creates what we want money to do for us.

When we are in the right place following our true direction, aligned with our purpose, we have fulfilment, contentment, and happiness. The energy around us is relaxed because we are doing what we need to do. We don't yearn for the stimulation of material excesses. Abundance, a feeling of being secure and joyful in our life, is a natural result of this. We can then live a state of being rather than being used by forces who are opportunistic. Let us begin to understand this more solidly by using ourselves as an example:

Example of a State of Consciousness

If you can grade your thoughts and the incidents created by them, you may discover there are times you are pure in your intentions to yourself and others. In those moments, you feel love, happiness, and contentment. This love overflows, and you cannot help but share with those around you. You feel like you are in the middle of your river flowing with life and you meet its challenges enthusiastically. You are accepting of yourself and your personal challenges, and you spread this goodwill to others.

These attitudes and intentions can initiate sensibility among others who may want to be around you during these times. Energy amasses without too much effort once it has momentum and can foster memorable events. Perhaps the ambiance of your aura and your attitude attracts others, who may want to perform some meaningful deeds with you for the greater good of all. How many wonderful movements of energy have been built from these compassionate intentions commenced from the spiritual elevation of one person?

> For where two or three come together in my name, I am there in their midst.
>
> —Matthew 18:20

To understand it even better, let us look at the opposite: When you are manipulative and deceitful in your thoughts, you may feel insecure and possessive of others. Relationships can feel burdensome and confronting, maybe even controlling. You may feel unhappy with this situation but be unable to find a solution to change it. This is like a living hell. Our energy is violated by confused souls, which we can become accustomed to and believe is our fate or worse, that it is normal. This is an unawakened state of consciousness.

By using our experiences as an example, we can determine the feeling of specific states of consciousness. In the first example, you are in a good state of being. You may feel like this when surrounded by the beauty of nature and you are free from stress and pressure. You may be alone in these environs or with others you have affinity with.

This is what energy experiences are like. When we relax, we can accept beneficial energy insights that help us generate some clear and focused decisions about our life and how to live it in a more relaxed-feeling way. If we are presently only experiencing this on holidays, we need to make a paradigm shift. The challenge is then to maintain it and our ability in this respect is what governs our state of consciousness. We can then, with a focus on refinement, make our life a heaven on earth. That is why meditation offers us profound healing. We take time out from our thoughts and allow our inner truth and its understanding of providence to regroup us. Surrounded by nature, it is easier to do this.

Opposite to this, you may have had some very ordinary thoughts, perhaps even criticizing yourself and others. Then you can compare, compete, or judge yourself and others. You may have hate thoughts or other negativity, which can then downgrade your energy and allow it to demean you, permeating it with contamination. All of this is happening as a very normal part of living life, but it is not normal, and neither is it part of our plan to live, other than to heal the forces that create this disharmony within us. We don't have to endure it but rather cure it with resolve.

> Madness is to think of too many things in succession too
> fast, or of one thing too exclusively.
> —Voltaire

At these moments of discord, we can become separated from our feelings, and we may start to yearn for outside stimulation. We may want to get relief from the hell we are living. We can be looking for what we can't provide ourselves—the ability to touch our feelings. We may, during this dark time, descend in our state of consciousness, which can even include depression. We can often subsequently mask this by artificial highs. We can then become addicted to the ups or emotional highs as a way of life. Then afterward it is usually followed by a down, which can take the form of an even deeper depression.

> I have lived eighty years of life and know nothing for it,
> but to be resigned and tell myself that flies are born to be
> eaten by spiders and man to be devoured by sorrow.
> —Voltaire

If we decide we want to live in a euphoric state, we can control the quality of our thoughts and aspire to live a higher state of consciousness. Learned behaviour can be a very addictive way of life. In due course, we need to be willing to starve ourselves of any habit-forming, negative attitude in our life. This is where affirmations play a central part in reprogramming our minds to work for us instead of against us. There is a website set up to offer this service, which I will be displayed on the back cover of the book. There are various affirmations for specific purposes. You can make them up yourself after awhile. Before I met my mentor, I used a book by Louise Hay called *You Can Heal Your Life* for this purpose.

Technique #9: Affirmations—to Heal Emotional Out-Of-Balance States

You can begin with:

> I choose not to live my life with concepts of _____
> (Can be hardship, negativity, judgment, or any other word
> that may affect you in your thought patterns) and rather

93

I choose to live _____ (now find the opposite of the word or words: a state of being, a positive consciousness, acceptance of myself and others, forgiveness, love consciousness, clarity, confidence, etc.).

Elevated State of Consciousness

We can aspire to be more like our angels.

In the angelic realm there is a very affluent state of consciousness maintained all the time. Angels don't have ups and downs, and their energy is constantly strong and purposeful. We can call this an enlightened state of being, which they have attained through evolvement and perhaps a lifetime or more on planet Earth.

We have the same potential as our angels, but because of our memory dilemmas, we have forgotten to be that way and are perhaps having a lifetime to regain some lost spiritual real estate. As we do regain it through loyalty and sincerity with ourselves, it will help us overcome our adversities as we power up with energy.

One of the fastest ways to do this is to acknowledge we are a soul living in a fantasy world. How many people do we know who are talking from their feelings in our environments and speaking their truth courageously as they perhaps hear most others decoying their way around it? How popular has the truth about being here on planet Earth with a purpose to heal us and move on to educating others become today? How many people are attempting to live that way?

As we begin to follow through with those types of shifts to our life pattern, the advantages can be instantaneous, far outweighing the disadvantages of not being liked by everybody. It is not that we want to express our truth at the expense of our career or isolation. As the desire arises, we can find an occupation that services our truth, whatever it is. We need patience with our spiritual growth; it is not an overnight miracle. It takes time for the words of wisdom to become our own. In time, with commitment, we can definitely become our constitution. Sharing our truth, saying what we mean, and meaning what we say is liberating. When we do this we are using our intuitive perception. We are going to be talking about these attributes later in chapter ten. People who are in balance speak their truth in this manner despite being accused of being rude or discourteous. Their energy is always powerful and respected. If you can, it would be constructive to find a prototype displaying these qualities, usually in a leadership role, and mimic what you observe works for him or her. This helps you strengthen your inner authority. Remember spiritually, it is better to be respected rather than liked.

By working smart with our intelligent energy, we can automatically begin to think like a spiritual energy being, and our memory of living this in time can come flooding back. We may commence to re-own our abilities, like being able to move in and out of our body and to heal ourselves by purifying our thoughts. (In the next book on this subject of our soul's constitution, we can delve into more detail on this, when we have absorbed and made practical the revelations at the level of this book.)

We can open to our feelings and let our superman inner self live true to his nature. The soul has no colour, no race, no creed, no language, and no gender. In this circumstance, "he" is used as for a term for convenience. We can relate it to the comic strip Popeye where eating spinach gives him superhuman strength. When we live our feelings, we literally expand our aura to become powerful and protective.

The main advantage of our aura expanding is to assist us to keep integrity with our purposeful direction and avoid being distracted by the trivia of life. If we do find we become caught up in any provocative type of negativity or social activity that drains our energy, we can detach ourselves from it and refocus our energy and be in the business of our purpose. Our aura naturally expands with this change of attitude.

If you are having difficulty with this, there is a technique that can really help us along. It is called the Cutting Energy Technique.

Technique: #10: Cutting Energy

o   Lift your right arm above your head on the left side. Curve it and bring it down on your left side to cut energy from your left side (imaginary strings) as far down as is comfortable to reach

o   As you do, say, "I cut my energy from you _____" and say the name of a person or negative feeling like rejection, worry, stress, or whatever else that impacts upon your peace of mind or any other concepts, such as judgment, competition, manipulation, etc.

o   Now do the same with your left arm, bringing it above your head and down on your right side, cutting energy from your right side (imaginary strings) as far down as is comfortable to reach.

o   As you do this say: "I cut my energy from you (name the person)" or other words you wish to use.

o   Now spread your arms open in line with your shoulders, pointing left and right respectively (like a standing cross), extended fully and say: "I bring my energy back to me" while crossing your arms across your chest in a hugging motion. Hold still for a couple of seconds and really mean it. Hug yourself.

o   Now slowly unfold and open your arms again, this time pointing them up toward the stars and saying: "I open my arms to the universe." (This movement entails unfolding your arms slowly from the hug to point up to the universe in a V shape.)

o   Do this facing north, then east, then south, and then finally west. (Because we do it in a circular movement, we cut the strings of energy confusion create around us.)

o   Whatever you are having difficulty with you can apply this technique to. You need to change the words to suit your occasion.

o   It can be used for any circumstances in which you are having confrontation with others.

States of Consciousness in Review

We can furthermore talk about states of consciousness of places, countries, cities, suburbs, or regions, whatever words are familiar to you. Whatever way the big picture of a country is sliced up we can use as an example for the ascending and descending states of consciousness. We can use leadership examples in governments, corporations, or religions, matching them to the system of states of consciousness. The universe is the same. Government zones descending can commence as a country and then be carved up according to tradition into regions, then maybe states, then cities, and then communities or townships. Alternatively, if the language is contradictory, you can substitute the words yourself by using the priorities in your country.

#1: may be called federal or national or country
#2: may be called regional
#3: may be called states
#4: may be called cities
#5: may be called suburbs or rural areas
#6: may be referred to villages or communities
#7: may be small rural townships

The leader of #1 is comparable to the president, prime minister, king, elected party leader, or other of a country and has to have a larger spiritual picture than the person who runs a village or township. It will go down the scale with #2 (a leader of a region) having a smaller picture than #1, a president, etc., and #3 will have a smaller picture than #2, etc. Of course there are always exceptions to this, particularly when we the people elect say a president and/or the equivalent because of our greed. Then he/she will have a smaller picture possibly than what is required for the opportunity. When his/her actions backfire, we may blame him/her for his recklessness, but we, the people who elected him/her, need to do the soul searching and learn the lessons from it in particular. We the people always have the power, and we elected him/her in accordance with our out-of-balance ideas and for his/her ideology, which supported this.

The leaders of the states in the past may have sown some good traditions we can inherit when we are born there. Perhaps some indigenous leader inspired his tribe or community to a higher state of consciousness through his example and sharing. Because of that today the people born there generally think outside the square, as this spiritual leader did. Some of the American Indian leaders are often accredited with doing this. The reason we are looking at these examples is to compare this system to our states of consciousness.

When we change our state of consciousness, we alter the way we view our life. We make a paradigm shift. One day we observe the world in a certain way, and then we change to a completely altered perspective once we elevate our level of awareness. It becomes more expanded. We understand a bigger picture of existence than we sensed was available previously.

Picture we are the leader of a country, perhaps a president, a king, or an elected party leader like a prime minister. We have to encompass all of the awareness of all states of consciousness of the people we govern if we wish to be successful. We can't afford to be emotional about what people are thinking about us or influenced by it. We can't be overly preoccupied about our partner and his/her confrontations or even children and their challenges in life because we have the responsibility of a whole country and its commitments to meet and to deal with on a day-to-day basis.

We have to deal with the leaders of other countries, thus embracing their cultural preferences and prejudices. Therefore, our vision as a leader is always growing bigger with each day's exposure. We can't waste time on trivia. We have to hit the ground running and be flexible. We have to work with diverse people who become like a new family for us because we share most of our time with them. We have to take breaks, short ones to regroup, thus allowing us to keep our decision-making fresh and to stay as relaxed as possible within the opportunity, facilitating our communication with our guidance.

We learn to rely on people who are our advisors and they on us for big picture direction. We have to place faith in our communication with our angels because without it we will be lost. There is no one who has the ultimate responsibility except us, hence conversing with our guidance has to be intimate and timely, even if we don't know it is our angels we are seeking counsel from. They don't mind because like us, they want the job, our purpose, performed effectively. If we do that, we are accumulating a grand scale of spiritual real estate.

We have to be prepared to learn about ourselves because everyone else will be observing the details of all our deeds and chronicling them, as will history. We have to swallow our pride and expand beyond our prejudices. We need an enlightened state of consciousness and to be detached from others' opinions or the desire to be liked. We can allow ourselves to be spiritually elevated in leadership, which is a lonely place to be.

If we are not the leader but rather one of the people being led, we can have a very clear idea in hindsight of the leaders who had good communication with their guidance and those who did not. The ones who were social and talking nonsense and deceiving us we know were not connected. Those who got drunk on the power of the opportunity and were playing games, misusing it for their own advantage or stimulation, we can say they were in their ego self, not their connected self, and were imposing flaws in their own aura. They will in their evolution need to address those shortcomings with all those affected by their actions. Acquainting ourselves with this helps us identify the state of consciousness that we have.

How do we use our time? Do we hit the ground running each day in a relaxed, big-picture perspective, loving life and our opportunity to live it? If so, our future may be as one of these leaders we are describing. This is the biggest question we can ask ourselves. If we are caught in the following state of consciousness or at least some of the time, then the opportunities to change the status quo are endless and exciting. Adjustments in our life attitude, with a little propagation of truth, are going to be incredibly profound in comparison to what we are living now. It will appear miraculous, and all you are doing is sourcing a drop of your omnipotence.

Unawakened State of Consciousness

As we have already covered in depth, when we are unawakened, we are very stressed and anxious about many situations in our life. We have difficulty finding solutions by ourselves to problems. We don't like to take responsibility for what is happening daily, therefore we tend to blame others for our problems.

Because life presents such difficulties in this unawakened state, we can refer to it as hell. A great majority of people may be living this on planet Earth partially because of ignorance.

Emotion is the predominant characteristic of this state of consciousness. We can be oblivious to others and their needs, totally self indulgent, selfish, and indifferent or compulsively helping others while leaving out our own desires to become subservient to their whims or be robotic in how we live our life, afraid to change our situation because of the anxiety we have. We may be very fearful of authority figures, believing we have no voice against their will. We can live the life of a victim, always feeling as if we are beaten up or put down verbally by others. How would one imagine hell to be? When one has no inner peace, this is an appropriate description of hell.

Hell is empty and all the devils are here.
—William Shakespeare

Awakening—to Being a Student of Life

When we awaken, we look at the world with a transformed perspective. People around us may remain at the same level we were at before we were awakened. When we begin to pursue our expansiveness, the changes we undergo can be challenging.

Those who have not awakened may want to know what is wrong with us; we are weird or out of sorts or out of tune. We know innately it is because we are in a consciousness out of their reach spiritually. They don't perceive life as we do, and it may seem cumbersome to educate them if they have no ambition to alter their perspective. They are still in the old space regardless of how much affinity we had with them before. Rather than fall back into our maze, we have the opportunity to move on or at the very least direct them how to educate themselves as we have done and allow them space and opportunity to make their own decisions.

We can begin to undergo experiences of affinity with people who maybe we never liked before but perhaps respected. Or we meet a new circle of friends conversant with the way we feel about life now. This is how our angels assist us to upgrade the energy around us—everyone is coordinated spiritually.

This awakened stage has many levels to it. Awakening itself is on the first stair of the pathways to enlightenment of the student. Some people may consider it to be the highest level of attainment even though it is only at the level of awakening, the first of seven steps to acknowledgment of our soul reality. It does have that atmosphere attached to it because where we have transcended from becomes obsolete in our reality. It is the beginning of our journey with inner peace, which increases as we start climbing its stairs.

On this first of seven steps, we can perceive life transformed with more awareness. As this grows, we then begin to be ambitious in our new state of being. We may become more involved with our life and want to experiment with new ways to live. Ambition for this pushes us up the ladder of acknowledgment. It is at this stage we may be attracted to public speakers, particularly motivational and others. We are looking for inflow. We may be attracted to invest in a huge library of books on spiritual subjects of interest. We seek to collect intelligence because we are yet to learn it is within us. We are looking for echoes for our inner truth that is stirring within. Some of the direction we find makes a loud and resounding playback sound. Others we may play with and move on from after a while. We can go through many fads and phases, according to people around us, but we are doing research on what echoes and what does not, which is a commendable investigation of our truth. It is a special time, and as we improve our attitude to life through the example of the people we are inspired by, we are learning more about ourselves.

As we settle in to this newfound freedom, we may start probing for more clarification to match our new rhythm. These encounters with our truth may help to push us up the ladder of awakening even more as we begin to action its results. When we languish on a level, we often live delusion to make our stagnation more palatable. I have witnessed this with many people on the pathway to illumination, and suddenly an intellectual alternative presents itself and they take this easy road to nowhere, only to end up in the same place again with the same decisions to make. Many new age spiritual style religions are intellectually based and promise us the world of enlightenment with new age words to inspire us. Unfortunately in these circumstances we swap one dogma for another and perhaps better the devil we know than the one we don't.

Most of the spiritual courses available, regardless of the names they have, are usually delivered at this level of awakening, equally as this book addresses. That is because it is where most of the searchers are seeking wisdom, and it is where we can truly benefit from guidance. There are specific courses I mentioned I was given to accelerate this process, which the website (for address of website see back cover) will be able to explain adequately. Without our own investments, though, nothing will make us shift our consciousness. These are tools, not total solutions. Finding the pathways back to our inner truth can be the most challenging undertaking of this lifetime particularly without the availability of techniques to move our feelings, our growth maybe slow and inhibited. We need in these circumstances to tackle our pride. Generally we don't believe we have any. It is good to remember if we have an ego, we have pride. If we are truly humble in all situations, then our pride will be minimal. Pride is the first big stumbling block to our spiritual growth, and regrettably, in my experience, its invisibility is our greatest enemy.

> Generosity is giving more than you can and pride is taking less than you need.
> —Kahlil Gibran

Taking steps beyond awakening and moving through to acknowledgment of being a soul is at least a seven-step process on these pathways. Often as we embrace new, advanced ways of living our life, we may believe we are knocking on the doors of heaven because we have developed spiritually but in terms of what is available, or what there is to reclaim we have barely left home. This, of course, is good news because heaven as we approach it becomes our elevated celestial sphere.

The reason awakening is where we meet the biggest challenges is because we have to acknowledge our soul part as a player in our life and give up the power our intellect has possessed for such a long time. It is not easy at first. If you have questions about the state of consciousness you are living, we can make it even easier to discover with the following brief explanation.

Me

If you are living a *"me"* reality that is being very absorbed in yourself and what you want in life—and at the same time needing others to support you for this, that is the awakening level. This is because you simply have to cancel your obligations to others in life to learn about yourself. It is paramount to your growth you do that too. It requires us to invest in loyalty.

Awakening is a good name for the beginning level of this state of consciousness. As we explained, it is the first of seven pathways to true acknowledgment of our soul consciousness.

You can have a *"me"* selfish vibration in the unawakened states. It simply means you are unaware there are people around you who respectively have needs because your sensitivity is not opened to this reality at this moment and you are therefore cruising through life living with a blindfold on. Sometimes being unawakened is like being a bull in a china shop. We don't have the refinement to handle the good china.

You can say you are not yet at the awakening level when you live for everyone else at the expense of your own plan. This can be displaying an unawakened state of consciousness, which opening to self-loyalty can help you expand beyond. Sometimes it may involve a small obstacle blocking this expansion, and when you adjust it, you can accelerate your unfoldment.

Until our foundation for awakening is built as a solid pivot point, we can be oscillating between an unawakened state and awakening. A child under seven can help stimulate our awareness of the process of this first step of *"me"* awakening. As they explore their new environment, everything is focused around their survival, which is contingent upon our attentiveness. They are very loving, but their demands echo self-loyalty in its purity with themselves in the centre of their world. This self-loyalty is unquestionably their strength. They can be generous, but it is at this stage usually experimental. Their steps of awakening to their earthly identity are pivotal to the rest of their life, and we usually enjoy watching them "discover themselves," dismissing any concerns of our sacrifice for the pleasure of involvement. This is an apt description of awakening. We are on a mission. Of course, as we observe in this metaphor, the closer we are to the age of seven, we learn to include others in our world as we prepare for our age of reason. Similarly, as we approach acknowledgement, we know we need others to assist us to instigate our purpose.

Technique #11: Daily Keyword Technique—to Expand Your State of Awareness Beyond 'Me'

This technique may help you accelerate spiritually.

One of the best ways to expand your growth spiritually is by using a very simple technique.

o Each morning when you wake up—almost as soon as you open your eyes—ask for a keyword, the first word that comes into your head, and write it down.

o Now if you have trouble receiving the keyword, do the Clearing Technique (#7 in chapter five), and then after you feel relaxed, you can obtain a keyword.

o Have a notebook beside you throughout your day and write down impressions about the keyword you have written down (more than one is okay, of course).

o Suppose your keyword was "crystal." You might wonder what that would mean to you as you go to your place of employment. You close your eyes and try to gain a picture or a thought or an inner knowing or feeling about the word.

o Write down these impressions.

o As you travel through your day, allow your word to travel with you. If you break for morning tea, instead of doing the social thing, take a little quiet time for yourself and sit and reflect on the word. Did you have any revelation? For example, were your thoughts clearer today? If so, how? Write it down.

o As you travel home, if you are on public transport, again take time to reflect on the word. What does it mean to you now?

o Any time you have a chance, it would be productive to work with the word, gain impressions, and write them down.

o If after a while one word is not enough, take two or even three. You can make sentences with them or phases. Expand on them.

o This is one of the most powerful ways to accelerate your growth spiritually. It focuses your awareness on yourself, your thoughts, and your actions. This is the essence of soul-discovery.

It is pivotal you don't intellectualise your refinement, particularly in attempting to prove it to others, because this can delay your growth. You can mistakenly follow these decoys instead of actually acquiring it. It is time wasting, and time is precious. Refinement will come with exposure to your soul constitution naturally and at your own individual pace, a process of delivering you to you that has nothing to do with anyone else. Attempting to please others or compete with them is an unawakened state of being. You have to make yourself the king of your world in sincerity. Kings who have learnt the expertise of leadership do not tell their subjects their secrets because this can attract manipulation. Respect your timing. It sometimes may require a change of settings to facilitate the opportunity to have a relationship with yourself.

We do what is necessary for our path and purpose. If we put our true purpose on hold for the sake of others, we only delay their spiritual growth too. Each of us is coordinated in energy. When our timing for an altered life direction comes, everyone around us is similarly undertaking their own unique episode of this alteration at their level of consciousness. It is all in sync. We have to trust that we don't need to "play God" in our life script.

Until we are ready for spiritual changes, the idea may seem unappealing to us, and this can be because its timing has not been born yet. We can't see the pathway clearly ahead of us, but that is part of the plan. We have to learn to rely on our inner truth and its backing from our angels to guide us in the universe. We have no eyes to see with, ears to hear with, or touch to assess with. Too great a dependency on these senses can dilute our potential.

We can't ask others to show us the way either. Unless we are working with a trained spiritual consultant operating with a system of a predetermined profile or consultation that your guidance has cleared them to give you, it is virtually impossible for others to tell us facts about our destiny. At best they can make an educated guess. Spiritual courses backed by spiritual energy are the only system I know that works with truth. The courses must not tell us what to do but provide energy for us to receive clear messages from our angels. Profiles can help us find out what is blocking our sensitivity or why we are having trouble. An explanation of these will be on the website (see back cover for address). Our angels want us to invest in learning to talk to them personally, not giving others authority over us. It goes against the system of Spirit. They respect our wisdom; consequently it is crucial that we develop our sensitivity. Spiritual courses offer us our next step spiritually. They help us grow through awareness of how to use our sensitivity. Our potential is to reach our angels' state of being. We are always in training to redeem this purity.

If you are wondering whether or not it is difficult to find the pathways back, in my experience, the next step was always there waiting, but sometimes I needed a helping hand to find it. If I depended on some other person excessively, they would disappear from my environment. This is because we must learn that we can't make another person's truth more legitimate than our own because it invites manipulation and control between people. We can have the humility to listen and learn from others, but what we accept as part of our own constitution is entirely our responsibility. We can't blame religions, schools, parents, teachers, gurus, or any other form of instruction we receive, because we have our own inner truth to discern their suitability to adopt as ours or not.

Often messages for us can come through people who are good at channelling but who have little awareness of what they are saying. People strong in the perception of prophecy often provide this service for others. We don't have to share our intimacies with them. They are merely channelling and don't need to know our personal information. Sharing in courses or group work is different, positive, and healing. It is a safe environment controlled by our angels. The more honest we are in these circumstances, the greater the depth of healing we attract. Our angels set these environments for us to redeem ourselves through regrouping. Once we break through to our truth at this level and refine our energy, moving on to a new state of consciousness, we will not care about these intimacies because the pain is healed and we are renewed.

The Next Seven-Step Level of Consciousness—Internship: "Me And You"

Finally, after a seven-step climb up the pathways of awakening to acknowledgment, we cross the bridge to the business of life. We begin to want more purpose in our undertakings. How we manage our time becomes a more demanding consideration. We question our beliefs about life and can be philosophical the higher we climb up the level of internship.

In the meantime, because we feel the strength of our changes, we can become a bit dogmatic in sharing our beliefs with others. It may be a religion or a cause or other preoccupations. We are on a mission to gather understanding and we may impatiently take whatever is on offer. It may not be the right direction for us, but we give it our heart and soul. This level is often referred to as B-Zone, as we have been talking about previously in its out-of-balance state. It is the in-balance state of consciousness of this zone we are now revealing.

It is the *"me and you"* focus. I consider "me" first, but I know I need "you" to be successful. Sometimes it's all about *"me"* being the hero or other times it's all about being devoted to "you" because you are the king, expert, genius, mentor, or other authority figure that one aspires to be like.

For convenience we can call this state of consciousness one of contradictions. It is like a two-sided coin: apprentice/master; student/ teacher; devotee/guru; employer/employee; leader/follower; minister/ parishioner; and any of these similar relationships we have with ourselves first and then with others.

We can swing between the two roles very easily. We can with some people be a guru and with another a devotee. We want to lead an opportunity; we commit ourselves to study it as a devotee, and then we are sure through this dedication we will become the person we most admire and step into the guru, minister, teacher, or leadership role.

At this level, we can be unsure about what it is we have to offer. Sometimes we feel confident in our knowledge. We have acknowledged ourselves building a firm foundation, but now we need to learn its skills. We want to impart it with a teacher vibration because it is the vision we have of our spiritual landscape. Other times we are very unsure of what we know, we may then devote our time to learning it from some person or institution we place on a pedestal. We often become very hooked on advanced education at this level and may do many diploma or degree courses consistently that we may not need or use in our lifetime. These endeavours can be the result of our desire to refine beyond the student mentality.

This is often referred to as an internship level of consciousness. At this time, though, we can become very bigoted about what it is we are learning about and very bewildered. It is like being on a train track that is only going one way. There is little flexibility in it. We are not very open to new ideas out of our realm of self-understanding at this level of consciousness.

As when we talked of B-Zone, we mentioned the reliance on dogma instead of using the beauty of our intuition to guide us. There is always the temptation to be out-of-balance this way while we ascend the levels in internship. In balance we are learning about what a benefit our journey of enlightenment is to us. We then want to build a life around it. We learn to balance our two natures to have a bountiful life. We scale up the mountain to live benevolence toward others and ourselves and be the ultimate philosopher. Most of the famous leaders throughout history were at this level of consciousness. Those more philosophical were at the higher levels of internship because they were more "connected." Those more dictatorial were living their own dogma at lower levels of internship.

When we are in this state of consciousness, we are building a career with our wisdom. What is our avocation, and how do we want to live it successfully intertwined, if possible, with our profession to make our life more purposeful? The main focus is learning to balance our thoughts and our feelings in the business of living our life. Having a thought for every feeling and a feeling for every thought helps us manage our contradictions.

This level of consciousness is all about business. We are doing the business of our profession on planet Earth, which can in some circumstances be in lieu of investing in our spiritual purpose. This is always the challenge that presents itself. We may become a bit of an "-aholic"—that is a sport-aholic, shopaholic, workaholic, etc. We can be a bit overzealous in our pursuit of business, sport, education, or religion, living in the business of it but perhaps at the exclusion of all else. In these intellectual states, we may feel driven to exclude ourselves and our true feelings from our life and become obsessed with an "ideal" style of living. We will in these situations have a disproportionate use of our time invested in pursuits that do not pay energy dividends. We do not have a balance in life. Any use of our time that does not include allocation for soul-discovery is out of balance.

In the past where we have lived organized religions, we have had through following our beliefs a more balanced life style than exists today in refined societies. By devoting either a Saturday or Sunday to our religious worship, we were honouring our spiritual needs at this level of consciousness. We were gaining inflow, and at the end of the service or worship, we usually had outflow with other parishioners. We may have over invested or indulged during the week in excesses of life's offerings, and at the weekend we had the choice to stop and regroup our week. We generally used the occasion to spend quality time with people who were influential in our life. We helped them regroup or they helped us regroup, and we entered a soul-discovery energy day. Shared meals with extended family or community may have offered us quality outflow, satisfying an innate need to realign ourselves with our purpose of healing dogma or misleading ideals. Spiritually rubbing against others and exchanging dogmatic ideologies can help us enlighten ourselves to a higher consciousness perspective. In rejecting their dogma, we are forced to reassess our own.

Today with communications becoming noisier, the opportunities to relax into a self-regrouping have become scarcer as people change their habit patterns. Many substitute good-quality community gatherings for watching television. Perhaps it is one of the most influential mediums for spreading disinformation about the soul and its journey. Families become hooked on trivia and misinformation and pursue, as a result, time-wasting activities. It can control how people spend their money and use their time, and it has very little spiritual input.

> The television, that insidious beast, that Medusa which freezes a billion people to stone every night, staring fixedly, that Siren which called and sang and promised so much and gave, after all, so little.
>
> —Ray Bradbury

The Internet, although it contains a great deal of contamination and little control, can still offer us a more-advanced opportunity to communicate our truth. The reins are in our own hands, and we can turn off a computer easier than a television set and choose what we want to learn about. It is more of a one-on-one situation rather than controlling a whole atmosphere, as a television does. As we can change quickly spiritually, we can alter our perspective in an 180^0 turn, it is therefore best that we remain anonymous on the Internet, lest our words of the past sting us with their lack of refinement in our sophisticated future.

We can share our enterprising nature in a variety of ways, have feedback, and make adjustments in our attitude. We can participate in communities, which can help us feel less isolated as we recognize others have the same issues as we do. The deciding factor in the advancement of our spiritual growth is always going to be through our exposure to others sharing about their truth. We learn through the reflection of our own inner truth moment by moment. We can change our mind, as this disclosure can educate us to climb the stairs to a greater consciousness.

> Science urges us to occupy by our mind the immensity of the knowable world; our spiritual teacher enjoins us to comprehend by our soul the infinite spirit which is in the

depth of the moving and changing facts of the world, the
urging of our artistic.

—Rabindranath Tagore

It would be remiss of me here to cowardly avoid mention of prison
systems. People who fall into this dark place and attract this kind of
punishment have, for their part, usually lost spiritual control of their fate.
(At any moment, they can win it back through self-reconciliation. Planet
Earth rules will bend to spiritual rules if the need arises). I have had an
opportunity to witness firsthand the debilitating effect this archaic system
of governing has on a person's energy. As we support this system, we show
our true unawakened realities. People who want to see others punished
instead of rehabilitated are living the out-of-balance concepts of this zone
of consciousness, believing in right or wrong. We cannot play God here
on this planet, and if we attempt to do so, we will invite the same karma
that we are inflicting. It is good to remember, "As we inflict, likewise will
we be afflicted." The laws of planet Earth do not negate our own eventual
self-assessments. It is our crimes of the heart that we are here on planet
Earth to mend. If you don't wish to remain in the "red" on your karmic
balance sheet, never pass judgments on others.

There was a recorded quote from Jesus Christ that is an apt description:
"Let he who is without sin cast the first stone."

Chapter Eight: The Third Level of Consciousness, "Mastership of Planetary Concepts," "You And Me"

Knowing others is intelligence; knowing yourself is true wisdom. Mastering others is strength; mastering yourself is true power. If you realize that you have enough, you are truly rich.

—Tao Te Ching

The next level of consciousness equally with the other two mountains has many levels, but we can, for convenience of cognizance, use a seven-step approach. As the name implies, it is a greater slice of truth to ingest. We perceive life with a bigger picture yet again than the previous two. Each step is equal to at least seven steps of the previous level. We may no longer have the temptation to live dogma, as we now have the prudence of our acknowledgment of our soul part as a spiritual pivot point. We have graduated from the internship level and are purportedly becoming very conscious of ourselves and the world around us. We can begin to stand apart from the masses because we have more energy in our aura and wisdom lucid and articulate to share readily. We can be either taking some upper management roles or beginning to prepare for these undertakings.

This mastership level used to be the natural progression of most souls preparing to graduate from planet Earth to return to the universe making their transition back to the angelic realm. Unfortunately this is now generally only possible over several lifetimes because of the current state of consciousness of planet Earth.

Each of the seven levels is very distinctive, and the steps between them are very large mountains to climb in themselves. They do not come quickly for anyone, as we have to consolidate each level to break through its barriers.

This level is all about *"you and me."* 'I know you are important to my success, and when I treat you with conscientious endeavours and respect, I know life is going to be better for me.' We put the consideration and awareness of others first because we have understood and controlled our emotions, found the business of our life and its balance, and made decisions to assure our success.

This consciousness takes us to various levels of clarity as we are maturing spiritually. At this level, we begin to master the opportunity to run our own life, taking responsibility for ourselves. This generates opportunity to manage people, situations, politics, or whatever our particular spiritual expertise encompasses.

We want challenges but can be waylaid by competition. If we stagnate on any of the levels, we can be caught in procrastination, which we call limbo when we lose our big picture. We may limit our own growth because it is going too fast. We put our life in boxes or categories in this level of consciousness, but these boxes can only benefit us if they are moved around by each day's refinement. We can't be fixed if we want to stay balanced. If we keep repeating what we do each day, living comfort zones, our consciousness is more related to limbo where we sit on the fence because it is safe. We want to stay comfortable in our life with money in our bank account. We may have used our intelligence to reach this plateau, and now instead of crossing the bridge to self-attainment and putting our footprints firmly in the sands of time, we may be living off old investments.

If we hop off the fence, we can become hungry for more spiritual information and develop more ability with how to use it. We learn to be more a manager of our life. We can become totally committed to ourselves, and as we climb the level of consciousness of this mastership of ourselves, we usually enjoy a better lifestyle where we are more relaxed with who we are and can communicate with people in a more confident dialogue. Usually as we ascend the steps, passion to educate others presents itself, and we are acutely aware of how far out in front we have become. We may join communities or anywhere others can benefit from what we share to help them move along their pathways.

This is why we want the leaders of our countries to be at this level. Being higher up on the mastership level will enable them to deal with the challenges we may not even be able to visualize. At the seventh level, there is the bridge of commitment many have written about. It is where we cross over and make transition, but we keep our body. These people who have reached this rare state are very special and few. They have acquired the level of attainment that is like a heaven on earth, but before our ego tries to claim its place on the banks of the angelic realm, we must understand that it is where the greatest temptations are to invent our divinity rather than forge it. Those people like Mahatma Gandhi, the prophets and others of this consciousness shared their lives of breaking through these ascending states and arrived at the only truly identifying quality they all have in common, humility, because they know how little they know and are aware of the importance of the service they now need to offer others.

Many people can come upon the bridge, which does not mean they have crossed it yet, particularly if they merely acquire the knowledge of its existence. Angels show us the possibilities of what we can achieve spiritually only as we hit the lower levels of mastership. Awareness is usually to challenge us to prepare ourselves to cross the bridge, which requires a huge commitment. One can make many crossings. As one makes them, one takes another significant step to detach from planet Earth's misunderstandings. That is, we leave behind the concept of duty to the traditional ideas that have us expecting from others and we become more of service to their individuality and spontaneous to the needs of each of those persons who we enjoy intimate relationships with rather than following the crowd and bending our inner truth "to fit in." We release the dogma of planet Earth and enter a realm of giving, thus providing spiritual tools for others.

We live to impart our inspirations for the betterment of others. It is not easy to coexist in the two realms, and without adequate opportunity to outflow our wisdom, we can easily fall from the peak of the mountain to hit the bottom pretty hard. It is all about maintenance. We keep our thoughts in a space where they are as pure as possible and then turning our cheek when we receive ridicule or criticism. This is another fundamental characteristic of reaching enlightenment. We can't take people's opinions personally. We have to be bigger than that. Humility helps us take care of this ignorance, which our pride forces us to endure. We literally in this state of consciousness train to be an angel, which is called graduating from the earth plane. We deal with this in the next section.

As a symbolic precedent, some of the presidents throughout the history of the United States displayed characteristics of mastership as they sought to leave behind them their defining legacy.

Transition to the Angelic Realm: Professorship

When we finally cross this bridge or jump without a parachute into the gorge, we have found a heaven on earth.

> Come to the edge he said. They said: We are afraid. Come to the edge, he said. They came. He pushed them and they flew.
>
> —Guillaume Apollinaire

However, we need to maintain our state of consciousness, which we can do by learning the art of detachment. We are gravitating more to the image of our angels. We are graduating from the limitations of planet Earth. Life is abundant. We have reached the bottom of a magical mountain. To ascend it, we are always detaching and distancing our life from attachments of a planetary nature, such as ideas, ideals, whims, preferences, addictions, devotions, pride, greed, vanity, lust, sloth, gluttony, etc.

It is a great level of awareness to reach. Once we attain this reality, we can never play dumb again. We have to stretch our involvements to gain fulfilment. We have to perform notable deeds to leave our footprints on the sands of time. The number of people at this level of attainment is negligible, but we certainly can recognize them. They are those people we most admire—whose quotes we use for our own meditations.

They stand out in a crowd. They may have involvement in spiritual books, movies, or documentaries that move the masses spiritually, leadership roles with distinguished service for their fellowman, or humanitarian projects. They set a standard. It is probably because of their investments our planetary energy has reached the middle level of C-Zone or mastership consciousness. They bring with them the awareness of a greater awakening, and this helps people to aspire to learn more about themselves. Even if the masses are not interested in reaching extraordinary heights of attainment, they absorb the dialogue from the inspired people around them. Once we are ready to take the journey, we can discover it for ourselves and live life more enthusiastically. Whatever step we are on spiritually we can be a leader. One of the most powerful ways to lead is through example.

There is more to know about this, but it will be in a second book. It is too big a subject to do justice in a passing reference. There are other higher states of consciousness that deal more rapidly with our returning to who we really are, which is love.

We have to recognize once we are awakened our challenges grow bigger with each day. The goal posts must constantly be moving to accommodate our evolvement. We can't stand still or we will stagnate, which means we will go backward. This is not a good space to be in. Our next level of spiritual inflow is already available, even if we are not aware. Therefore, it is necessary to be flexible with what our guidance presents us and be spontaneous with it. Occasionally we have impressions to move cities and don't know why we would think such thoughts. If it feels stronger than our will to refute it, our angels may be giving us impressions to move us to a more genteel energy to match our new state of consciousness or to new challenges to help us grow spiritually. We may resist our true direction because of its growing pains initially, but the rewards outweigh the risks we take.

Our communication with our angels has to be the first priority in our life. Otherwise we will live theories about our spiritual reality. They help ground us. We can make them our most intimate advisors. A message for those who are advanced and singular in their communication with their angels: we have to be careful that we are not talking to clever but confused souls that we call grey angels. They exist, and many people are conversing with them. Although most often their intentions are not bad, they are confused, thinking they are our angels, though they really are not. Our angels never share any judgmental opinions of us. They are always supportive and diplomatic in a factual way. They do not share insights into others' lives or realities unless it affects us.

Our angels are not chatty or gossipy, as sometimes we may want them to be. They deliver messages to our feelings, flash us a picture if we are a visionary or give us inspired thoughts factual and brief if we are an intuitive. They show us a revelation that is felt as a lightning flash upward between our navel and our heart if we are prophetic, or they speak when we open our mouth to share, directing our conversation if our aura is clear at that particular moment. If we are a person of the feeling gift, we receive a gut feeling, which has energy, and a bad feeling if we follow the wrong direction. All of these impressions are downloaded to our feelings and gradually over time, these messages filter through to us if we missed the first flash. The reason they deliver in parables and symbols is to avoid educating confused souls about us, particularly grey angels. They do not broadcast our intentions and direction, thus avoiding confused interference.

Our angels always allow us to make our decisions; after all, this is why we are here on planet Earth, to learn and grow. We are in the planetary university every moment of every day, and all our thoughts, deeds, and actions, whether negative or positive, are all recorded in the Akashic records and available to us eternally. As we elevate our singular reality, we are grateful for this backing. Sometimes what our angels share with us is not palatable for our intellect; we may therefore prefer to find nice ideas to listen to. Grey angels are easily heard and give advice in an agreeable manner. But nice is not necessarily good for us. We have to instead substitute NICE: Need It to be Clear Energy (as an angel once shared with me).

We need to relax and not have anxiety about life at the level of awakening. Even if we do receive messages from grey angels, they are usually still relevant and productive to our life compared to the other messages we take direction from. We are getting inflow that we can understand. As we can be very attached to these grey angels, our angels help them gain enlightenment then they can truly help us. They often can be that wise grandmother or grandfather that we are following in the footsteps of or a larger than life ancestor we may have never met this lifetime. We can readily agree they have wisdom meaningful to share with us, but we can't believe they are God's messengers or we will limit our spiritual elevation. As we refine our state of consciousness, we are not participating in this dialogue anymore, and by now they have probably made the small jump they were hesitating with into the angelic realm, and in their absence, we can relate to our angels more readily. Many people in advanced stages of spiritual growth have believed they changed angels when a grey angel made their transition.

It is helpful to know that they do exist enabling us to become discerning about the messages we receive from our angels and from people we may be attracted to for the logic they offer us, but some advice they share may not quite gel with our soul's constitution. This is often indicative of the dialogue of grey angels. They have wisdom—but their counsel does not work out well for us long term. They do not realize that angels do not give recommendations because making decisions is pivotal to our self-training.

Angels give us options and explanations empowering us to make the decisions personally.

Elevating Our State of Consciousness

Apart from the obvious advantages of living joy, fulfilment, contentment, etc., we may ponder initiating changes to our state of consciousness, questioning the real advantages of their addition in our life. When we pass on and make transition, our energy vibrates at a particular level of awareness with or without a point to it. A point does not arrive in our energy until we are sincerely discovering our soul's constitution and following it, thus elevating our state of consciousness and driving our energy into, initially, several points. Our goal is to bring it to one strong point like a pyramid. The stronger the point, the further we can ascend into what we call heaven.

We do not need much imagination to visualize an airplane as a round ball and how difficult it would be to lift it off the ground and allow it to maintain flight using present technology. It is the same for us in the universe. Beyond our level of consciousness, the energy feels like concrete. We cannot penetrate it, therefore we cannot ascend beyond where we can vibrate. Comparatively, an airplane cannot break its speed barrier or optimization of flight it was built for.

There is a great incentive for us to seek a "Christ consciousness" when we have experienced a more affluent way of life in the past and yearn for a return to our true spiritual nature. A ticket to planet earth has the potential to change our fortunes from a poverty vibration to spiritual abundance, and we may be able to achieve it with dedication in one lifetime. If you recognize what you are living needs elevating, becoming aware of it does not make your life negative. On the contrary, it more often shifts a sizeable amount of the negativity blocking us merely by its cognizance. We can often experience this when tears involuntarily come into our eyes and we feel like crying. This (the crying of our Spirit) can be the energy of confused souls leaving. It is different from other types of emotion, which are more correctly termed crocodile tears. The tears in the first instance are real, and as is the shedding of confusion.

The following table of our states of consciousness may help us for a ready reference.

State of Consciousness	Focus	Zone	Out-of—Balance	In-Balance Experience
Unawakened	Me—indulgent	A-Zone	Hell	Awareness
Awakened	Me—discovery	A-Zone	Hell	Soul Acknowledgment
Internship	Me and You	B-Zone	Purgatory	Benevolence
Mastership	You and Me	C-Zone	Limbo	Commitment
Professorship	You	C-D Zone	Grey Space	Detachment
Educator	Spirit	D-Zone	Black Tyranny	Evolution

When we reach the higher levels, we feel a resurgence of zeal to assist the search of others. The training of ourselves as spiritual consultants is a challenging occupation because as each of us endures the changing fortunes of our purpose and the personal challenges we face, a spiritual consultant has a far greater journey to embark upon, with pride and ego being their greatest adversary in this pursuit and the rejection of their truth from those they seek to support. It requires diligence, humility, advanced sensitivity, and patience with the first priority, clear communication with their guidance.

Chapter Nine: Our Angels

If a man has an angel to whom one could listen once in a thousand times the angel would show him the way of uprightness.

—Job 33:23

In the angelic realm, there are angels and many of them. For convenience of realizing who they are, we can compare this dimension to our ideas of heaven, nirvana, utopia, and/or paradise. It is really our true home as well as the home of our angels, and despite not returning there permanently recently, we are definitely each of us undertaking a project to regain our divinity. The keyword to reach this large zone of enlightenment is, as we shared previously, detachment.

When we decide to come to planet Earth (that is, when we are in the universe waiting for an opportunity to incarnate), we first must choose a team of angels to back and support our journey. It is too perilous for us to come to planet Earth without angels, as we might move backward instead of forward in our zealous quest for refinement and waste a precious lifetime. The team of angels we ask (and who agree) to back us to move out the creases in our energy, we choose wisely.

They consent because they have perhaps had similar experiences and healed them or they love us and want us to be successful or both. For whatever reason (each person's experience being their own individual one), we have a team of angels who are backing us twenty-four hours a day, seven days a week.

They are always with us, notwithstanding we may not ever have acknowledged their presence. They are always on our side. We can equate it with the relationship between a criminal defence attorney and his client. The attorney is always endeavouring to fight the incarceration of his client, going out on a limb to ensure he enjoys freedom. Our angels always want the best for us. Even when we are negative toward ourselves, they are working to help us to understand our potential. They never reprimand us or agree with any of the judgments we endure from ourselves or others. Their dialogue is always supportive and solution oriented in times of challenges.

They are at least double our energy at any time, and when we are relaxed, they can come around us and add their energy to ours, which we can feel as chills or a warm inner glow or being lit up by energy. When they do that, we can often feel invincible and that nothing is beyond us, or at the very least confident to take on the challenges ahead of us.

They know all about us from the past, and they know the goals we have set ourselves this lifetime. They help us to be successful in achieving what we want to achieve (which is our purpose for being here on planet Earth). How can we fail with this backing and support? They are definitely living their enlightenment. Therefore, if we can copy them, which is part of the system of evolvement, possibilities are demonstrated for us to begin to live our enlightenment also. We become a reflection of our angels as we source our potential.

I have personally experienced numerous youth who grew up with the backing of a clear dialogue from their guidance, which they were using as their first priority in their lives. Even as minors, they had powerful, focused energy and were realms apart in sophistication and maturity from their peers. Perhaps this is a future trend for the next generation in the making. Unfortunately in maturity there was less demand for them to share their wisdom as their profession. They therefore entered corporations and/or began their own businesses, which they were ready to do at sixteen years of age, and most were very successful. Although their education was more of a spiritual content than intellectual, it was more than adequate to form a determined path to an abundant reality. They accomplish tasks quickly, and their minds are razor sharp. Boredom with the ineptitude of their surroundings may have been their only burden in life.

Really the only influence that can halt our success is our own inner dialogue (what we say to ourselves). This happens moment-by-moment because it is our negative inner dialogue, which hosts confused souls, which then drain our energy and make us emotional and unenthusiastic about our opportunities.

At first, because we may be trying to comprehend these many new revelations about ourselves, the reality of having angels may come as a surprise to us. If so, we may feel a sense of being overwhelmed in trying to absorb the value of it.

To help us understand how to build a relationship with our angels, we need to accept that they know the truth about us, all our secrets, but regardless of what we may judge about ourselves, they have nothing but unconditional love for us at all times. They can feel the struggles we go through, and although they could make life easier for us, they do not interfere because our soul growth and development is their highest priority. Because we choose our destiny by our actions or inactions, we are agreeing with whatever occurs here on planet Earth and the lessons we are having. It is difficult to imagine any other explanation when you understand the potential of our angels to intervene. Even if we are not at this moment aware of some of these possibilities, in time with the opening of our sensitivity, we will recognize exactly how we have overlooked all the clues to their true identity and why.

It is not wise to take our angels for granted. They are a gift we have that helps facilitate our spiritual growth on planet Earth. They are more powerful than any force you have met up till now on planet Earth. They can change the weather, change traffic lights, wake you up in the morning, and call your name if you have lost concentration or are in danger. Even if through interference you may be going to have a fatal accident, they can intervene. Of course, I feel sure they must account for their actions if they interfere inappropriately. It is not an investment they would make lightly. Besides, everything they do is coordinated. There are no mavericks in the angelic realm. They have even brought people back from imminent death. They have delayed planes, trains, or other transport if a person may have misunderstood their direction or been waylaid for some pivotal appointment.

They are powerful but powerless to make our decisions for us. It is best to consult them, even if we do not understand their messages to us. Be respectful of them always. They guide us to fashion our fortunes or misfortunes, which can help us gain respect for them. They have endless patience and compassion to help us find our constitution and our way back home. When we begin our discourse with them, life becomes magical and mystical. I call this the honeymoon period because it is comparable to those types of feelings in a relationship when we have recently found profound love. Imagine talking to a person or people who regard you as the most important person in this world and who want you to share your intimacies; they can then assist you to be happy and who believe in you more than you can possibly support with reality, offering you explanations as to why it is unnecessary to doubt yourself. How successful can you be? Is there a limit?

The love they have for us is amazing. It doesn't take us long to realize our life works incredibly well when we communicate and coordinate with them. They understand our language easily, but if we talk to them with our head and not with our heart, they will not be able to respond successfully, because unless we transmit with our feelings, it is not coming from us but instead from souls who want to manipulate us and the energy of our angels for themselves. They have endless patience to hear about the woes of our life. We can pour it all out to them and miraculously in time we can have a change of attitude. We can share disappointments, unfairness, abuse, loneliness, unsuccessful relationships, or anything we want to fix, and in time we will graduate toward a solution because it is their highest priority. We must trust that when the solution does arrive, we don't reject it. It may assist this recognition by sharing that in my own experience solutions seldom came through the doors I expected them to.

> Destiny grants us our wishes, but in its own way, in order
> to give us something beyond our wishes.
> —Johann Wolfgang von Goethe

As you evolve and desire to refine your relationship with them, it is best to converse with a sense of gratitude and humility. How easy is it for us to forgive a parent for not giving us our own way when they truly invested in our own best interests and prevented catastrophes in our life. Similarly, this is what our angels do. Examples of styles of communication:

> Please angels, I do not understand what I am to do in this situation. Will you please help me find what is in my best interests to follow? I am sorry I have not always trusted or understood your input, but I am learning. Please have patience.

This is your more your feelings talking.
The following is talking to them with your head.

> Angels I would like to win the lotto. Angels I would like you to arrange for me to have a new car, new job, new house, etc. Can you please let me know when to expect it?

A better communication if you really feel you desire a change in circumstances or certain projected desires to materialize in your life would be:

> Angels, if it is in my best interest, please will you back me to change my job if there is a better one for me somewhere else, or if not and it is in my best interests to remain where I am now because I am learning something or healing the past, please allow me to understand why? Angels, can you please help me find the abundance for a new vehicle because I need one for my employment?

Our angels do not back us to steal therefore it is prudent for us to remember the Ten Commandments in receiving answers. If people offer us gifts spontaneously they may be needing to repay us from a past life. That car we need which we believe is vital to our success may be their road to repay a karmic debt. Although your pride may inhibit your ability to accept, it is best you exercise humility and forgive them the debt in this exchange. When we begin to converse with our angel's strange encounters like this happen to us more regularly.

Our feeling nature knows all these refinements; we may simply need to relax with it and in time try out some communications with our angels. They are always listening to what we say to everyone, including ourselves. We can include them in our everyday conversations. We may be very surprised at how they respond. Don't be alarmed; it is a natural phenomenon. Because you didn't believe in them does not change the reality of their existence.

If we are asking them for advice or want them to run our lives for us, they do not react, because they respect us and are there to back our decisions, not make them for us. They will give us hints and nudges about what we are doing that may be the reverse of what is in our best interest. Usually if we ask them a question by saying, "Is it in my spiritual best interest to . . . or if you were in my position . . ." they will find a way to give us a reply. It is always best to clear our energy with the Clearing Technique #7 (refer to chapter five) before we do this. For example, we may ask them if it is in our best interests to date someone or become engaged or married. They do give us input, because it is pivotal to our soul-journey and discovery that we clarify accurately these types of choices we need to make. Our angels do know how to deliver messages to us. We have to trust their superior intelligence and experience. We need to relax and be patient and open to whatever means they choose. Meditate to make it easier to receive the "full" dialogue they send. Each message can have multiple levels of insights and inspirations if we allow them to.

As we alluded to earlier, our angels talk to us through parables and symbols. There is a very good reason for this. Confused souls talk to us through thoughts, emotions, and negativity. If we receive communications that are conceptual in content, they are never coming from our angels. Our angels may highlight signposts for us to read or bring us people to share insights with us, or direct us to books, movies, plays, etc., that can assist us to become more aware of our thoughts or attitudes that beg for refinement. This can be on a daily basis, if we are open to it. They may send us a favourite song or a song we happen to know the lyrics of. We may hear it again and again, and the words may seem to speak to us with solutions for some challenges we are presently living. People who have the first perception of intuition can often be drawn to music and hear their angels speaking to them in songs. We are about to talk about the four distinctive perceptions. People with the first perception of vision may find messages in symbols.

A picture paints a thousand words.

—Chinese Proverb

When we pass on, our angels are there to direct us to where we need to go. We wrap up our lifetime and regroup for three days, predominantly with our loved ones, and then we move out to complete whatever other tasks we can attend to, to fulfil our mission on planet Earth, travelling with the backing and guidance of our angels.

We can return to our loved ones whenever we are needed, and they will feel the energy of our angels with us. Therefore, our involvements with them will be positive and energizing. This is why numerous people conceptualize their loved ones departed have become their angels. It is such an amazing experience to have a wealth of angels backing your dialogue. We encounter our loved ones around us when we are thinking about our life with them. Incidents that are wonderful to remember and other events we may have forgotten that were difficult may then resurface for healing. Part of what their regrouping involves is explaining to us the occasions where they may have erred in their judgments and attitudes toward us. This way our recalling of these incidents can moreover help them heal their emotional misunderstandings.

We can forgive or ask for forgiveness for our own errors of judgment when we are ready to do that, and any past conflict can be resolved. You may feel some heart tugs at this, but they can then become our spiritual family in our next lifetime, one of those special people you meet who you befriend and life would never be the same without their friendship. You usually have your previous loved ones around you now as close friends. It is very necessary for us to have communication with our guidance or our real life will roll on without us being conscious of its consequences.

There is one interesting experience I did have with my departed mother, which I would like to share. My daughter was involved with others creating something that was my mother's specialty, and my daughter asked me if I could solve an issue as they were stuck on how to proceed. She commented, "I wish your mother was here to ask her advice," and in moments I began to channel my mother's response. My daughter commented on how much I sounded like her in that moment. Then after she delivered the solution and rejoiced momentarily, she left, and the feeling was wonderful and fulfilling. It felt liberating for me as she highlighted my experiences of her skill in picture form enabling me to clearly explain what she was showing me and thus share her wisdom adequately. My daughter was grateful, and my cup felt full.

Alternatively, if you are talking to a departed loved one who is confused, as we have shared before, it will be a draining, emotional, and perhaps a depressing experience. You may cry and feel sorry about his or her death. Whenever there is negative emotion, such as uncontrollable sobbing when we talk about a departed loved one, it usually means they are present and confused about their next step.

At times, people, when they wrap up their lifetime, if their learning has been very profound on planet Earth, they may move into the angelic realm and make themselves available to back others to do what they have done. This is called graduating from the earth plane. We can reflect that a person like Mahatma Gandhi (and many others) could have had this type of transformational transition, as did my mentor. Of course, there are many people who are still alive who fit this spiritual description, but it would not be prudent to mention them without first obtaining their permission. We can perhaps conceive they are people we know who are highly visible and admired by most people on planet earth. Nominees of the Nobel laureates often identify some of them for us. They often risk their life and their freedom to liberate others on planet Earth.

A small body of determined spirits fired by an unquenchable faith in their mission can alter the course of history.
—Mahatma Gandhi

When we are unaware of the enormity of a planetary opportunity and the potential to release us from our own captivity, we make transition the way we have described. When we are preoccupied about people or possessions we left behind, we can instead be looking down on planet Earth, yearning to remain there. We don't see our angels who are above us. We may try to return to planet Earth but this time without a body because we are ignorant of the repercussions of this. We are stagnating instead of wrapping up and regrouping enabling us to move onto a new lifetime, perhaps with the very people we are trying to interfere with.

When we become confused, our angels cannot help us because we are as they are. We have the same potential as they do. We cannot be told or forced to do what is best for us. We must come upon the rationale ourselves, or we have the free will to remain in a confused state. The same standards apply on planet Earth. No one can force us to comply with spiritual laws. They are not the same as planetary ones. We are a spiritual law, each of us, and when we work against ourselves, we have consequences, such as illness or disease, that can shorten our lifespan. We can become unenthusiastic and joyless. Our angels can't save us from our bad choices. If we elected to talk to confused souls and have our energy drained, there is little they can do about it. We may not remember the consequences of this behaviour despite innately being aware of it or our dogmatic ideas about it may overshadow our wisdom.

Chapter Ten: Our Four Perceptions

*Everyone may speak truly but to speak logically, prudently
and adequately is a talent few possess.*

—*Michel de Montaigne*

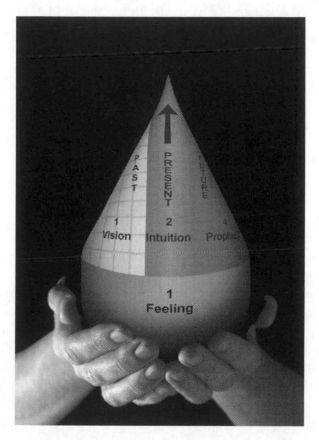

As a spiritual, inimitable, and individual being, we are capable of
communicating with the angelic realm naturally. Each of us has our own
distinctive style, using our individual perception to exchange messages
with our team of angels.

There are four perceptions or styles of communication. We have all four, and we naturally use them in a particular order. This order of perceptions gives us certain personality traits, which come from the persuasions of this particular order and how we have unfolded each of them, which governs how we live our life and how we communicate to others and to ourselves. Although there may be many on planet Earth who share our particular order of perception, they will not share the same encounters as we have. Each of our lives and their happenings are matchless, and early environmental influences will be exclusive and mould our personalities accordingly.

With this awareness, we gradually absorb the realization of our own uniqueness, and we can then accept the individuality of everyone else. This will make our life less complicated as we release expectations of others based on our learned set of rules. For instance, we may have fixed pictures about how life should or shouldn't be, and we may expect others to feel the same. But looking at it from an enlightened perspective, we find the acceptance to know that differences open opportunity for creativity and expansion. We learn from others. Therefore, why would we want them to be the same, thus inhibiting our opportunity to expand our horizon through interaction with others? Each person is like a book we have not read, and as we review the pages (or feel their aura), we learn new talents.

I would like to give you an example of this. A relative of mine is very creative, incredibly so. He is always drawing some new design. He regularly draws designs for relaxation. When I was involved in some projects with him of house renovation, I would receive these visual impressions from my angels of designs for the renovation. When I shared this with him, feeling pleased with the acquisition of my new refinement, the exact image, complete with many more details I lacked, he had already drawn on paper. This was confusing for me at first. Then as time went on, I realized when I changed locations the images disappeared and only reappeared when I was in the same location as him at the same time. This has now been my experience with many people.

One can simply listen in to the energy, and it makes for better and faster coordination for projects we are all jointly involved in because we are all on the same page. Our angels open up the window for us all to share insights.

We may want to ask, "What is a perception?" If we look at our communication system like a circular sound system with four speakers and four microphones, in different circumstances we use different systems, its explanation is more digestible. Each of these speakers represents a unique and sophisticated system of conversing that we own. It is how we operate as a universal being. Of course, this explanation is a very brief overview of a profound system that deserves more time and attention to details, but it is out of the terms of reference of this book.

Our first and favourite speaker and microphone is our primary means of conversing with our angels and others. We are alert and open to the world around us through its particular qualities.

Our second perception can additionally influence who we are very strongly, particularly if one of our parents had this perception as their primary one. If it is different than ours, we have possibly become used to communications in this way, predominantly in our first seven years. Because it may be a familiar form of receiving dialogue, it holds no mystery to us. When we hear others sharing about their perceptions, we can more often readily identify with the qualities of our second perception. If for example, our mother was a visionary we are used to receiving picture communications our particular sound system includes video. If our father was an intuitive, we would need to give the facts to him on all subjects regardless of how trivial or unnecessary they may appear. It is auditory thus making sound pivotal to successful delivery including volume, tone as well as content.

We often process our life through our first two perceptions and give little attention to the other two. It can be in discovering which of the four is our primary means of communicating that we can truly begin to open ourselves to receive messages from our angels. We are of course already receiving them, but awareness of the process can help stimulate more qualified meaning.

We can look at our four options and try to identify which is our primary perception. Sometimes because our parents can be very influential on how we process life, we may even attempt to act out their first perception instead of using our own. As you read on, you will learn why it is preferable we do not do this. For this reason, we have to be very discerning about which one is actually our first perception. We may change our mind many times until we know, and this is normal.

There is a spiritual profile one can have to determine this and how many angels we have in addition to receiving a communication technique, which takes the guesswork out of it. This is available in certain parts of the world (see the back of the book for details). In the absence of this possibility, one can open oneself to an awareness of each of the perceptions and therefore endeavour to determine which one is our first. By identifying it, we open prospects to learn more about ourselves.

Each of the perceptions has in-balance and out-of-balance qualities. It is imperative that we qualify how we converse. If we are not using all our perceptions in balance, we are living our life diluted and not having the breakthroughs we want to enable us to live our contentment and fulfilment.

Our First Perception

In order for our angels to facilitate the smooth delivery of their transmissions to us, they use our order of perception, the first perception first; video, audio, gut feeling or inner knowing. It can be like using the front door of a house to enter. Once we know which one it is, we can be militant to only recognize dispatches that come in this form to be sure we are receiving clear messages from our angels which we can base our decisions on.

Our Prophecy Perception

The first perception we are going to talk about is prophecy. It is our spiritual nature, and that has a very defined purpose in our life. Each perception, in addition to being a two-way system of conversing, serves other essential purposes in our life. Each of them also has a colour.

Our prophecy perception is where we receive an inner knowing, and because it is our spiritual nature, it particularly likes to know about the future. Prophetics don't know how they know the information they share; they innately know.

- o They may know tomorrow they are going to meet someone for the first time and this person is going to be very influential in their life.
- o They may know which political party is going to win an election. They may even know by how many seats.
- o They may know when they come to a new area where to find valuable services like restaurants, banks, and supermarkets without ever being given direction as to where to locate them.
- o They can often drive to places they have never been before by following their inner knowing.

Sometimes prophetics may seem to be a little strange. It is these qualities of knowing the future that can make them appear to reside there and perhaps be a little out of sync with their surroundings. Other qualities of particularly young prophetics can be their ability to sleep through episodes of learning or movies or other opportunities to inflow information, and when they are aroused from their sleep, they may remember the details of all that happened in their immediate location even though they appeared absent. They can be very skilled at sitting for exams because they use their inner knowing to unfold the answers they are looking for, like turning the pages of a book ahead to read the future. Prophetics have a profound sense of taste and smell and can be attracted to professions involving these senses. They can be very keen executives when they are confident in their inner knowing. They can quickly grasp the big picture of situations and for this reason can be good at delegating to others.

Prophecy is one of two sensitivity perceptions. Two of the four perceptions are sensitivity and two are planetary. That means they function contrastingly. A sensitivity perception doesn't have a picture or words. It invokes a type of sensing. In the case of prophecy, it is an inner knowing, and in the feeling perception, it relies on gut feelings, which are actually very different. A prophetic's grasp on events unfolding is immediate, while gut feelings take time in acquiring details, which is slow and precise. A person of prophetic perception often goes into a trance-like state, which looks like daydreaming.

A prophetic has to rely on his ability to discern his feelings in order to retain the balance in his life to function in the big picture of his perception. Unfortunately, many prophetics, because they are unable to discern, can live the out-of-balance of their perception, which invokes manipulation and control of people and situations. Because they know their own insecurities, if they cannot discern, they can easily recognize these uncertainties in others, and this may make them want to control people and environments to their own advantage, using their executive insights in a negative way. Once they trust their discernment of the immediate future without needing reassurance, they can return to the extraordinary qualities their perception can offer them naturally.

When dealing with prophetic children, expect the unexpected. They love shocking you or surprising you. It is very necessary for them to express their creativity. They can be wild and untamed because they dislike repetition and get bored easily. Allow them to express themselves. You need quality time with them, and it will pay dividends. Encourage them to share their stories. Expose their attempts to manipulate and control their environment. The colour of prophecy is purple. Many prophetics wear this colour obsessively enabling us to easily identify them in a crowd.

The following technique can help us identify with the perception of prophecy.

Technique #12: Our Prophetic Perception

o   Remember a time when you were driving a car or daydreaming and you could not account for some minutes or even hours of your time.
o   This is how your perception of prophecy works.
o   When you are strong in the perception of prophecy, you can go into a trance and travel time dimensions.
o   Because this perception is open to receiving pages from the future, you can receive an inner knowing or hunches about what might happen today, tomorrow, or in the future.

o   Close your eyes and ask your guidance to give you an insight, using your perception of inner knowing of a situation that is or about to unfold that is relevant to you.

o   Organize it into the following structure by using these keywords:

     What: What is the big picture of your impression?

     When: When is the timing of it?

     Where: Where is it happening or to be directed?

     Why: Why is it necessary, or what is the why of it?

o   When you have the impression, spend time on it until you understand it. It can help you recognize how you use your inner knowing.

Our Visionary Perception

The perception of vision governs the clarity of communication. It focuses on social interaction and exchanges with others in our life. It is our social nature, which in this age of expression is a big part of our life. Understanding about our perception of vision can really help us to live our social energy in-balance because the out-of-balance can be very destructive and time wasting.

This communication is through forming pictures in the mind's eye. These pictures are the impressions a visionary person receives from his or her guidance. It can be transmitted in a flash. Visionaries can operate their lives from the pictures they receive without even being aware they have any.

It maybe inconceivable to visionaries that anyone could live without a picture, imagining everyone has one to guide them. Visionaries are very particular about the beauty of their surroundings. They usually love nature and want to make their surroundings beautiful. They are more often concerned about the impression they are making on others and can be eloquent in their speech and fastidious in personal attire deliberately, thus ensuring they are visually appealing to others.

They can often speak expressively, describing the picture they see in their mind's eye. They are very visual people. They usually have empathy and feeling for others and are able to read into their pain and feel the need to support them. A visionary can see into the soul of a person through their eyes and may refuse to conduct business deals until they meet all those involved in person. This is the perception that is skilled in order and organization plus symmetry and balance. Visionaries can be very adept at making plans because they refine what they see into categories or boxes. As they visualize the process, they can readily picture the final result of a plan, and they naturally strive for the perfection of it. Because of these qualities of their perception, they are solicited to plan and manage projects and people.

Visionaries can have a photographic memory and recall the details of what they see in picture form. It is usually very liberating for a visionary to find out about the attributes of their perception because it clarifies their uncertainties, thus avoiding the judgmental side of their out-of-balance characteristics.

The visionary perception out-of-balance can breed many energy disturbances. Visionaries can strive for perfection to the exclusion of all else. This may put them in direct conflict with others. They may believe their picture is the only one, and once it is fixed in their mind, they can have great difficulty changing it or being flexible to permit input from others. They can judge people and situations, being tormented by their own ideas of their inadequacies, and this can make them feel depressed and isolated. They can then source illusions to try to make their fairy-tale life more palatable. In dealing with children with this perception, avoid criticism of them and always find diplomatic words when dealing with discipline. They do not lack conscientiousness. They learn quickly. Because they have an active imagination they may find TV or movies terrifying and endure nightmares as a result. They are prone to fixed pictures and thereby need gentle care and concern to alter or modify them.

In balance, a visionary person is a planner. They can excel with the attributes of their perception when organizing chaos into refinement. The colour of the aura is yellow. People with vision as their first perception more often have a very cool aura, whereas the other three perceptions are warm. They may feel the cold more than others as well. Because energy is concentrated through their eyes, they are often commented on as beautiful. We can call the visionary perception the big, big picture. Nothing much can happen successfully without a plan, and it is our visionary gift where our strength of organizing and planning comes from. We can relate it to CEOs, developers, managers, architects, engineers, graphic designers, interior designers, artists, and many more. They usually have a very developed visionary part, even if it is not their first perception.

The visionary perception is endlessly creative. Even air traffic controllers are using their visionary gift for planning the successful order of flight movement. We use our visionary gift for a certain type of memory when we take photographs of learned material, and we recollect this way. Because it is a planetary gift, it is more liable to be influenced by analysis instead of spontaneity of decision-making and vacillation instead of confidence of movement and plan construction. It is an important perception that we all use regularly in our life for success. Knowing its strengths and weaknesses can truly help us navigate our way through life more confidently.

Technique #13: Our Visionary Perception

o   Close your eyes and visualize the house, apartment, or residence you live in.
o   Without looking around you, open your eyes long enough to write in a notepad your description of what you saw.
o   Describe it in detail.
o   Go through each room with your eyes closed.
o   Close your eyes, and then with them open and lowered, write a description of the room you are in now.
o   Ask yourself if you saw a picture or if you were working with your inner knowing, feeling, or a memory without pictures.
o   You can do the same with your refrigerator, visualizing its contents.
o   Try to work with a picture in your mind's eye.
o   Be patient to allow it to form.

Our Intuitive Perception

This perception is your business nature and is possibly the most misunderstood of the four perceptions. Many people believe they are this perception because they have what is popularly referred to as intuition. If they instead substitute this misused word intuition for sensitivity, it can relate to all the perceptions.

Intuitives hear their angels. They have a very good thinking mind. Because they are acquainted with discerning thoughts, they can often know the difference between clear messages and confused ones. For this reason, they make great leaders. It is as if they can in a flash of insight interpret communications for others to help make them become successful. For clear communication, one needs to develop some inner authority, thus facilitating the ability to direct confused thoughts and confused ideas others may want to involve us in with an abrupt rejection.

Instead of engaging in worrying about hurt feelings their communications may engender, intuitives more often go straight to the blunt facts. This is a quality intuitives have that is often misinterpreted as rude or abusive, but it is a very valuable attribute because it keeps them and others clear of confusion of catering or entertaining ideas that dilute the natural progression of business.

Intuitives can excel at leadership of others and complete projects by keeping others on track. They can be very impatient with people who are disrespectful of themselves or others and are usually not reserved in sharing their feelings on this regardless of the attitude of others. It may only involve a few words; the message is loud and clear. Their energy is powerful and directed when they have all the facts of a situation and they know why they are involved.

There are usually fewer intuitives in any environment than the other perceptions because of the leadership qualities, thus making it easier for one of them to assume leadership of a group. If there are a number of intuitives, once they decide who is leading, they make good followers. They are usually the preferred perception for leadership of people because of the natural attribute of their perception. Because they are essentially fair and honest in their dealings with others, they are usually well respected, an important characteristic in good leadership.

There are several people who displayed these qualities in the leadership of the United States such as Abraham Lincoln, John Kennedy and Benjamin Franklin. This shows a good range of differences in the styles of leadership, but each of them was primarily leadership oriented. There are numerous other intuitive leaders, of course, but it is good to recognize these qualities of leadership and how they may relate to this perception. We can identify with Mahatma Gandhi, whose real journey of enlightenment and leadership began with an incident when he and others were shown disrespect.

For example, Winston Churchill was more prophetic with strong visionary qualities. He was an outstanding executive, delegating opportunity to others to lead with a sense of detachment but with a real ability to make decisions under pressure. He was a great orator and motivational speaker, with an uncanny knack for knowing and channelling the future. This was a great quality to have for the type of leadership needed at that difficult time. When the situation changed and the people desired another specific type of leadership, he fell out of favour. George Washington, in my opinion, displayed more visionary qualities. He had a very big picture and had empathy and feeling for others that was important for the planning and management of a new country. He knew where people fitted best with their opportunities. John Adams appears to be more prophetic, with great insights into people and the future, which were cornerstones of his leadership.

The intuitive perception out-of-balance can make a person very hostile and aggressive. Even at times in elevated leadership opportunities, they can display the qualities of a dictator. Although an intuitive is unable to handle pressure, he may unyieldingly apply it to make others subservient to him. He can be good at making people nervous of him to gain control of them.

Intuitives out-of-balance can alternatively be very introverted, showing little or no leadership at all and making sure that others are unable to read them or be aware of what they are feeling. They can swing between these two out-of-balance qualities of their perception. Often an intuitive person has a deep and/or loud voice, which commands respect. It can be difficult to gossip with an intuitive in balance who only likes to lend his/her ear to facts and who dislikes trivia. Intuitives pivot their lives from gathering information on a whole range of topics beyond their field of involvement or influence. They are very fair and feeling with people displaying the traits of a feeling perception person but with boundaries and usually with no real love of details.

In dealing with intuitive children, always make sure that everything you want them to do is their idea. If they understand a situation, they will co-operate. Force will only destroy their respect for you. Gauge the authenticity of what they are sharing respectfully. Even as young children, they can be incredible leaders and channel their angels. It is vital for their voice to be heard and heeded. Respect is the keyword in dealing with them.

The colour of the aura is red.

You can do the following technique to identify this perception more clearly.

Technique #14: Our Intuitive Perception

- o   Remember a song you heard that you liked.
- o   Go over the song in your head, remembering the lyrics.
- o   What does it mean?
- o   Are the words a message for you to be aware of?
- o   Write it down.
- o   Meditate on it.
- o   Ask your angels now to choose another song for you to work on.
- o   Take time to identify it.
- o   What are the lyrics?
- o   Write down what the message is you are hearing from your angels.

o   How does this feel?

o   Are you hearing your angels or seeing the words and music or following an inner knowing or a feeling?

o   How comfortable are you with this technique?

o   Will you use it often?

Our Feeling Perception

We have not yet described the feeling perception. This relates to our personal nature and is the second sensitivity perception. It is the perception that heals by touch. It is the feelings in their raw state without encumbrances. Therefore, it can offer us a very keen way to learn about our feelings, observing how we or other feeling persons act spontaneously without analysing when the perception is in-balance.

This is an extremely sensitive perception. People with this as their first perception are usually very caring. They can feel others' pain and can become very involved in trying to heal them. They can sense energy through touch. They are often engaged in talking gently and caringly to others and touching them as they do. They are usually very affectionate, and the happiness of others is pivotal to their enjoyment of life.

They often find negative situations overwhelming and difficult to linger in because they are unable to detach. People with this as their first perception like the details of labour. It keeps them out of their head when they have involvement, particularly using their hands in manual labour. They usually have good coordination skills and manual dexterity. They can build energy of places and make their engagements fun to be part of for others because they love to participate and this is contagious. They can find endless satisfaction in working with details of any profession they are involved in. They can be patient and precise, working slowly and deliberately.

When they are out-of-balance, they often have difficulty distinguishing their own feelings from those of others and may even feel others' physical pain as if it is their own. Their energy is very high and moves laterally across the planes of planet Earth. They can lack a buffer of detachment for themselves because of this as they soak in the negative energy around them.

They usually make wonderful doctors, nurses, naturopaths, social workers, psychologists, community leaders, or any other of the healing arts. They often love to be involved in massage or any other opportunity where they can use their perception of touch for healing. It helps them regroup themselves as they outflow love through their hands. They will often go out on a limb for others and have to guard their very high energy because it is certain almost everyone wants a part of it.

When they are out-of-balance, they can become emotional and overwhelmed by negativity. They can have difficulty distinguishing between feelings and emotions and may feel powerless in situations where they are criticized. They can play a victim to try to control or manipulate situations and gain attention from others this way. It can be an out-of-balance way to seek love.

In dealing with children of this perception, it is important to always give them hugs, more particularly if they are angry. It helps them realign their energy. Children of this perception have great difficulty in intellectual societies. They sense energy and can feel everything around them. For this reason they may be misunderstood. They share the details of the details because every facet of their life is important. They are closer to their feelings of love naturally than the other perceptions and are usually well liked by all. They need a stable loving home environment to be able to thrive in life.

If they had difficulty finding love early in life, they can become very intellectual and pursue professions that are very mentally demanding and spend most of their lifetime feeling separated from their feelings. People with this perception fare far better if they are able to keep a blank mind and allow their feelings to direct them in their life and to keep busy.

It is a tremendous advantage to be able to feel one's way through life without taking direction from thoughts. Because feelings are not as popular in many intellectual societies, people with this perception can feel isolated from the mainstream and may strive to be outstanding intellectuals. Given their ability with details, it can often be easy to realize this. They may become expert lawyers, but it may be at the expense of living their purpose if they did not come to work with this. If they did, they often direct their talent toward humanitarian considerations, fulfilling their need to heal others. Robert Kennedy showed strong traits of this gift.

The colour of the aura is blue. The nature is our personal.

Technique #15: Our Feeling Perception

o   To awaken your feeling perception, find an object to hold in your hand.

o   Choose an object you feel has energy. Choose discriminately.

o   It may be an apple, a piece of paper, a stone object etc.

o   Write down whatever it is you feel when you hold it.

o   Feelings may take longer than the other perceptions, necessitating a patient attitude while waiting for the information to come.

o   Describe any other feelings you may have about it, particularly in the past. The feeling perception has a great ability to read the past.

o   If you want to, you can while holding the object put healing energy around whatever you are sensing needs healing.

o   Are your hands warm?

o   If they are, then they are probably in healing mode.

o   This is a trait of people with the first perception of feeling. Their hands heat up when they touch people to heal them.

o   While your hands are warm, if you can, find someone who needs healing. Often your hands for no apparent reason can warm up, and you may question why. Then someone close by needs a healing. Place your hands on this person till the heat vanishes if he or she permits you. If it is a headache, you can place your hands on the area where the pain is.

If we are new to the idea of using four perceptions, initially we only begin to learn about our first perception. This is normal and appropriate. In time with practice and experience, we need to discover our other three perceptions. Our angels will have the timing for each of these steps. While reclaiming our truth in all these areas, there is a technique we can do to refine the way we converse by making them embody a what, when, where, and why.

Technique #16: To Balance Our Perceptions

One of the fastest ways to help us to learn to keep our perception balanced is in using a technique that can facilitate the definition and refinement of our communications where all our battles for the discovery of self are won or lost.

o   Go over all the challenges (including difficulties) you had with people over the last week. If necessary, you can expand it to a month if you have not many or decrease it to a day if you have too many.

o   Now write down what you feel you experienced. Write it like a story.

o   For example, write, "On Wednesday of last week, I had a very difficult communication with Joanne about work I did for her that she was not satisfied with. I felt very angry and then became very upset about it."

o   Once you have finished writing it down, put down the following words in this order.
What
When

Where

Why

o Now take what you have written—your story—and put it in a "what, when, where, and why." For example:

What: Unresolved/ emotional communications

When: Wednesday last week

Where: Over work I performed at the office.

Why: Because I felt it was not justified and became angry and upset.

o Now that you have it broken down. what part of it do you want to work on?

- Is it your reaction that is the problem?
- Is it your work that is the problem?
- Is it Joanne who is the problem?
- Is it your anger that is the problem?

o Meditate on each of the questions and get a feeling for which one needs work.

o Now to work on it. Let us say you choose number two.

o You then can meditate on your work. Why was your work a problem?

o Were you rushing? Is Joanne very critical, or is she simply more discriminating than you are?

o If she is more advanced, then it is great, as you have an opportunity to improve yourself by learning from her. You may instead, whenever she criticizes you, show your willingness to upgrade your work. It maybe that you have your pride, an inherited confusion that we explained before, which you don't want or need. In these circumstances, it is best to swallow it, work on humility, and be patient to find out if it will change the situation. If not, it is not really about your work.

o If she is critical in an unreasonable way, ask yourself why.

o Is she this way especially with you or with everyone?

o If she has an attitude to only you, has she always been that way, or is it only recently? If the answer is that she is always critical toward you and your anger is an emotion that surfaces around her only, now you possibly have a past life that you are healing.

o The next question you may desire an answer for is how can you get all this out of the way.

o There is an effective and easy technique that you can do to heal past lives or generally difficult situations with others. This technique helps you open to your true love energy, and as you do solutions, become available.

Dangerous is wrath concealed. Hatred proclaimed doth lose its chance of wreaking vengeance.

—Seneca

Technique #17: Healing Inflow and Outflow, "Inflow Acceptance Outflow Love"

o Stand and place your feet slightly apart, hands by your sides.

o As you do this, you now, raise your arms to shoulder height, and in a sweeping, outward movement, you spread your arms open wide.

o You now bring your hands to your chest, and as you do this, you say out loud, "I inflow acceptance of _____." (In this case Joanne.)

o Now you slowly and deliberately extend your arms again outward at shoulder height, and this time you say out loud, "I outflow love."

o Repeat this a few times till you have it in your feelings.

o When you do not feel any more emotion between you and the person you were having difficulty with, you can take it further and say:

"I inflow forgiveness of myself and Joanne. I outflow unconditional love."

o If you do this several times maybe over days, weeks, or even months until the energy between you and her changes permanently, you may have avoided a difficult lifetime with her as your mother, father, sister, brother, or even as your child.

This is more often how we heal past challenges with others by being thrown together with them in an intimate and healing circumstance, like families.

It is a great investment of time to do this technique with everyone with whom you have unresolved issues. You can merely change the words to fit the occasion. The bonus of this technique is that we are all energy and the love energy that you are sharing transmits at the speed of light. You can therefore say Joanne felt the changes, and given time to assimilate them, will make positive adjustments in her attitude toward you.

Now when we do the four 'W's' technique, we are breaking up communications into our perceptions to organize as follows:

- *What* is for our prophecy.
- *When* is for our vision.
- *Where* is for our intuition.
- *Why* is for our feeling.

By doing this regularly, we are refining our perceptions. We are usually pulling them out of the mess of general disregard to instead develop a respect for each of them and what they can offer us.

Prophecy, as we know it as our spiritual nature, provides us with the big, big picture of our life and where we are going. We can call it our spiritual perception. We use it to visit the universe at night. On planet Earth, it offers us insights into what is ahead of us in our life, the overview.

Vision is the organization and planning of our life on planet Earth. The when is therefore meaningful for our success. If we are too far ahead or behind, we will not have success in life. Our timing needs to be succinct. We want plans to make our life flow with symmetry and balance. We innately realize the people we have involvements with and the timing of this.

Intuition is all about where to direct our energy. It is the business of our life. We point to where we sense our focus or energy can most benefit our life. We give direction to others and ourselves. We gather facts. We gather the illuminations and inspirations of our opportunities and make it the business of our involvements.

Feeling is all about the why: Why we do what we do. Why we want to be involved. Why we are on planet earth. Why is as much about looking backward to remember, thus avoiding making the same mistakes as we did in the past, and facilitating a refinement of yesterday's astuteness.

To make it simple for us to understand, this following table may help:

Perception	Communication	Nature	Colour	Answers Question
Prophecy	Inner Knowing	Spiritual	Purple	What
Vision	Symbols	Social	Yellow	When
Intuition	Connected Thoughts	Business	Red	Where
Feeling	Gut Feelings	Personal	Blue	Why

The Fifth Gift: Evolution

There is a fifth perception that is barely on the planet and may take a decade or more to be a permanent addition, but for those who are more discerning, it is an important revelation. This perception is involved in the process of evolution. It answers the question who. The colour of the aura is a type of maroon. It can be understood as the process of evolving beyond planetary concepts to the ultimate reality of love.

People who are sharing their love with their fellow man can show us the strength of this perception. People such as Mother Theresa have displayed some of the qualities of this perception. Its overall focus is love. Her deeds showed her to have embraced her true unique vibration, which is for all of us, love.

Chapter Eleven: Our Purpose

How strange is the lot of us mortals! Each of us is here for a brief sojourn; for what purpose he knows not though he senses it. But without deeper reflection one knows from daily life that one exists for other people.

—*Albert Einstein*

We can call our purpose the reason we are here having a lifetime on planet Earth. Many people want to know as they awaken what their purpose is.

It is a difficult question because our purpose changes as we embrace refinement and move up the ladder of states of consciousness. In the *"me"* mentality, it is our opportunity to heal our past. This is our purpose. We may wonder what there is to heal. The answer to this will be in your early years. What were you unhappy about? Sometimes we bury these experiences because we want our life to appear perfect. But if it were perfect, we would not be here on planet Earth. We have to dig deeper to find out how we may have denied our inner truth to please those in our early life. Ask yourself, "What do I love and hate about planet Earth?" Make a good list. Once it is made, ask yourself, "How does this symbolically relate to me?" When you have the answers, you know what you need to heal within, and as you do so, healing will happen around you. What you love you have already healed.

To reveal your inner truth is an integral part of your purpose. Your inner truth grows larger and wider with exposure. At first, little challenges of sharing what we feel work wonders for healing the "me" mentality. But as time and awareness march on, the goal posts shift and we have to accept bigger challenges as more of our truth is revealed to us.

Our angels do not divulge more than we are ready for, and they seldom foretell our future. We may have come to make great changes to the planetary consciousness. I certainly hope so, as it can use all the help it can recruit. But before you can do this, your personal healing has to be solid. As we shared before, this is your personal energy. How has it been contaminated by your intellectual ideas of how life should or shouldn't be? Ask yourself how often you are annoyed or angered by situations. Anger is a strange emotion; it usually has little to do with what or who it is directed at.

Anger

One easy way to find out about our anger is to find out what makes us angry. In what situations are we angry? Is it to do with our partner, children, siblings, other relatives, or friends? We may be angry in the traffic but at certain people or with strangers we have never met before. This is a typical example of shifting the blame.

To give an adequate example, in our early life when we work against our inner truth, we feel anger with ourselves for doing that. We do this because we feel pressure, usually from one of our parents or other role models in our first seven years, and we may decide with the maturity of a three—to seven-year-old that we have to modify our natural behaviour to be loved. We then can blame this influence and in particular those who participated unconsciously in making us work against ourselves. We want to fit in with our parents and siblings and be loved and accepted by them. We often make compromises to do this. Then, as we mature, if we have not resolved this anger, when people with the same energy present themselves in our life, we take our anger out on them.

Each man is the architect of his own fate.

—Appius Claudius, Roman Statesman 300 BC

You may wonder what I mean by "people with the same energy." There are many people we meet in our life who have a similar energy feel as our parents, siblings, etc., and we are drawn to these people because their energy is familiar. We often marry people with the same energy as our mother or father particularly if we do not feel loved adequately by one of them. We may then be more attracted to finding love with someone of the same energy as the parent we felt rejected by.

Unfortunately, as time goes on, more often than not we will undergo the same problems with this person as we had with our parent. People with the same energy usually behave the same way toward us, and inadvertently, we help promote this as they play their script in our relationship with them with the same lines as one of our parents, we predominantly act out our part in their life as one of their parents. As the gloss or honeymoon wears off, we may feel the same yearning, insecurity, or rejection once again (whilst they may experience the same frustrations with us as they did with one of their parents). For much of our life, experiences of this are repeated because we keep magnetizing the same type of people to rebuff us. Eventually we will resolve our differences amicably by healing them within, a positive result, and/or we will find people with the same energy as our other parent and our relationships with them will be more constant, even if less exciting.

The anger we feel that is buried within us has to be resolved. This is the friction we talked about earlier that inaugurates the format for change. Even if it does not feel good, it is good for us, particularly when we do not have the awareness to choose our own adventures down the pathways of redemption in coordination with our angels. Marrying people who we have stormy relationships with and who force us to stand up for our inner truth can actually help us mature spiritually. Therefore if your days on the psychologists couch to heal yourself do not embody this realisation, your investments there in endeavouring to understand yourself may bear little fruit.

If we want to change the tone of our relationships, forgiveness of ourselves is the best place to begin. We forgive ourselves for working against our inner truth and realize our parent did the best he or she could and we chose him or her for that particular reparative gift. This is a good

outcome for everyone. Ignoring it can send us to therapy for too long, and until we address it, there may be no great sequel to our life's contentment. This is, as we have explained before, because of past lives. We will find the true route of all anger is self-betrayal. Shifting blame lifetime after lifetime compounds and delays our opportunity for inner peace.

Patience and forgiveness are the antidotes to anger. We can do the Inflow and Outflow Technique #17 (refer to chapter ten) and amend the words appropriately to, "Inflow forgiveness of myself and outflow patience with myself."

These are the type of challenges one faces in the healing of one's *me* mentality. It is a noble purpose, and until one is done, one cannot really move on spiritually to the *"me and you"* mentality, which is the business of our purpose.

The Business of Our Purpose

To live the business of our purpose, it is necessary for us to learn the difference between our inner truth and our programming. We can call our inner truth the dialogue of our soul and our programming the dialogue of our intellect. By now I am confident you will agree there is a great disparity between them.

As we have shared extensively, our intellect is the part of us that sits in the driver's seat of our physical vehicle, our body. It is the eyes and ears necessary for following our direction. Our soul does not have eyes and ears but has resources—sensitivity, memory, discernment, intelligence, and direction. Our soul part says where the vehicle goes and what engagements are our opportunity when it arrives at each destination. Often because of our intellectual misunderstandings of who we are, we can give up the power of our resource, our soul power, and then our driver can be influenced and distracted by the activities around him/her at the expense of us giving him/her direction to follow our soul's own true purpose in life.

> Unhappy is the fate of one who tries to win his battles and succeed in his attack without cultivating the spirit of enterprise, for the result is waste of time and general stagnation.
>
> —Sun Tzu, Chinese General 500 BC

We are driven by an innate force (magnetism) that we require a quiet and subservient mind to follow, which comes through our first perception (e.g., an inner knowing, picture, inspired thoughts, or gut feelings). To use a metaphor, picture yourself trying to write a thesis on a subject in the middle of a party. This is often the scenario of what we live and the environments we choose to expose our soul part to live in and to try to communicate to us. It is perhaps comparable to a whirlwind of thoughts thrown around like a stew; it becomes difficult to identify the ingredients.

In these impossible circumstances, we can't feel our purpose because we are all caught up in the distractions around us. Others can influence us, at the expense of our own unique purpose and its direction. Others, in turn, can become affected by us at the expense of their unique purpose. Possibly if this happens to most people, we can generalize and say everyone will become directionless and purposeless. Sounds a bit like planet Earth on a bad day. People may generally be following a good career or a money trail instead of investing in what feels good to do.

o   But at the end of their life, is it really going to add up to qualities they can take with them such as wisdom?
o   Or were they driven by a concern for survival or greed?
o   What are the real spiritual scores on the board?
o   Or is it the possibility of another wasted lifetime to add to an already cumbersome score?

These are valuable questions we may want to include in our goals and targets if we desire to attain inner peace and contentment.

Some Spiritual Truths

Planet Earth is not a social destination. Neither did we come here to build physical structures at the expense of our metaphysical needs and direction, other than what our purpose dictates, because nothing lasts. We can't live here. We can only visit, and we don't have control over where we may reincarnate. Therefore, continuity of the fruit of our investments is not assured. Next lifetime, we can't claim bank accounts of cash or assets left in our old (past life) identity because no one will affirm our ownership. We have no physical proof of this identity. If we have not healed our differences with our family, we may possibly reincarnate on that line again, and that could be on any continent and more likely with those we still have difficulty with.

There are other planets we have perhaps had lifetimes on. Planet Earth is not the type of a planet that can offer souls reincarnating the opportunity to relive a continuation of their old life. It is more like a day trip planet. Whatever is here is to use and return and to respect, thus vacating it intact for the next guests (generations), which may be our children's' children and/or their children, who may or may not be us. We can enjoy the opportunity of visiting planet Earth and be ready to move on when it is over. Even if we put our whole lifetime into building monuments physically, they return to dust or compost eventually, like all planetary life and its structures, including us. Most constructions we build only last for a short time after our transition. If we equate it in eternal days or years, it is nothing but a speck of dust in the eye, removed quickly as an obstruction. Therefore, what is the value of such pursuits?

Using a metaphor to understand this, conjure up a vision of yourself sitting on the foreshore of a beach and building a giant sand castle for everyone to enjoy. As you labour in its construction, you fantasize everyone is going to read about it, enjoy it, and acclaim it as the biggest or best they have ever seen. Then the tide comes in and it is washed away, it becomes merely your memory. This is symbolic of what can happen in each lifetime. What you build only endures for a short time beyond your domicile here, and it disintegrates with age. Few of your structures in the physical sense last beyond a couple of generations.

Ask yourself, "What of the past have I erected that I now am in awe of in this reincarnation?" If you do not remember any of your past lives and you view your life in a big-picture perspective, where do you desire to make changes?

What remains for a short time after us are our deeds of self-conquering. Everyone who left a legacy of enrichment for others in our history began by prevailing over himself or herself. Self-mastery is all about self-discipline and self-control. It is saying no to what is not our opportunity and focusing, at the expense of being unpopular, on what truly matters, which, of course, is staying in the stream of energy provided us . . . living its healing, otherwise termed living our soul constitution. Our purpose is much more fun to live than any opportunities our duty can invent for us. It is where our fervour lives, whereas some people source out passion in obscure and adverse ways involving countless confused sex spooks when they are off course in a compulsive way, which gives them little animation and dubious obsessions they become shackled to. Sex spooks are people who pass on confused about love, believing it has to do with intercourse between two people—having only regard for this act and not the person they are sharing it with. There is no energy backing for us to live duty, mass consciousness values, dogma, or greed, yet day after day, year after year most of us are doing that.

> We forfeit three-fourths of ourselves in order to be like other people.
>
> —Arthur Schopenhauer

It is not that we have to change much to live our life plan—merely our attitude. Then we need to be courageous with any changes that may present themselves as necessary. The direction of our life path and purpose is mainly living where our focus needs to be, and this usually is on healing ourselves, first taking time to do that while living our life's opportunities fruitfully. Instead of our day being repetitive and without challenge, we can make it resolute by healing past lives with the people who we are working with. This is happening automatically. We feel it as disagreeable. People who don't like or respect us or people we prefer to avoid appear to make our life difficult. To clarify the facts, we can source keywords each day. Our angels will provide these if we relax and allow their inspiration to flow through us. It is a more fluent way to live when energy backing us to live our destiny literally carries us through our life. We do not need to invite criticism by sharing our intimacies with others, although we may be bubbling with the enthusiasm of these encounters. No one else needs to participate. All of this is achieved through working with our angels. If others question you, direct them to "how you found your pathway," not revealing your personal experiences of it to avoid future manipulation or ridicule.

Technique #18: Keyword Technique for Emotional Situations

o   If you are confronted about a situation or you feel emotional, find a quiet place and do your clearing technique.

o   After you have done it and you feel relaxed again (give yourself time to do this—feelings take time to relax, and there are no trophies for speed in this endeavour). It is more a meditative form of energy. You have to relax into it. If it is difficult to find a clear space to do your technique, you can visualize it and ask your angels to clear your energy.

o   Repeat it until you feel chills, goose bumps, or a warm inner glow. When you have the feeling, ask your guidance for

#1. A keyword to explain your situation. Make a sentence with this keyword.

#2   Ask for another keyword to go deeper and make a sentence with this.

#3   Ask for a third keyword and make a sentence with this.

o   If this is showing you insights on the circumstance, write down discernments on what you believe it is.

o   You can work on this until you have some recognition. You must stay relaxed and keep a calm, quiet mind.

o   After you have a feeling for this, ask your guidance for

#4   Another keyword, and make a sentence.

#5   Then ask for another making a sentence for each word.

#6   Then ask for another keyword making a sentence.

o   Now put the first three-keyword sentences (#1, #2, #3) together in a paragraph, which is an explanation of the problem.

o   Then put the last three-keyword (#4, #5, #6)sentences together in a paragraph, which is an explanation of the solution.

o   Meditate on it and write down any insights.

o   Now you have the big picture you can keep going with asking your guidance for keywords until you have a feeling for what you are receiving.

o   Thank your guidance and ask them for backing to heal your emotional reactions.

o   Do not lose your sheets of paper but rather write them in a notepad you keep for your communication with your guidance.

o   As time goes by, look at what you have written maybe in a day or then again in a week and then again in a month. Each time there may be more and more insights for you and changes in your life to regroup.

Technique #19: How to Meditate

To meditate, you may not really need a course in meditation to learn a technique that works for you. If you already have one that is working successfully, don't change it. For those who haven't meditated, the following may help.

o   Close your eyes and relax. At first the phone may ring or people may call out to you. It may appear there is a conspiracy to try to pull you out of the meditation. Recognize this and make arrangements to find a way to bypass those distractions next time. You can trust how meaningful it must be for you to learn to meditate if all of those distractions try to stop you from doing it.

o   It is beneficial to find a suitable safe atmosphere where you are alone and you can then begin to meditate more easily.

o   Allow all the thoughts that first surface without becoming frustrated, and persist in washing them away, getting a clearer and clearer silence each time.

o   Maybe visualize being on the seashore, and each time your mind is full of thoughts you don't want, they appear before you on the sand and the next wave washes them away.

o   Use your keyword for the day to keep a focus, and as thoughts come up, turn down an imaginary radio knob or turn off the television in your mind.

o   Persevere. It may take time to find silence, but remember that you can meditate even with all the traffic in your head and feel renewed.

o   Whatever you do refines itself with each involvement, it is therefore necessary to invest in persistence. It is like the saying 98 per cent of success is achieved through turning up. You keep on keeping on. Each day that you do a Keyword Technique you are living your purpose in some small or large way.

o   Be patient with yourself. You are retraining your feelings, which are slow, precise, and methodical.

The traffic in our head, which interferes with us meditating, comes through our intellect and the pollution it has picked up. We have power over this. We have to take back the controls of our life from our intellect and empower its direction from our feelings again.

When we do this, whatever we live becomes quality time. We may have a conversation with a friend or neighbour and become enlightened by its symbolic nature. We can prepare a meal and feel abundant from the opportunity and success of it. We can dig a garden and feel like we have the world at our feet as we sow our seeds. We can vacuum a floor and feel grateful for all we have been given. We can change our life and everything we do from mindless vacillation and even bitching about how we spend our time to being meaningful and grateful. Always ask your guidance for a keyword before you embark on any opportunities.

This is truly living our purpose. As we develop good habits, our purpose can expand its terms of reference, and we may suddenly be mastering other talents we did not believe we had.

Remember, our life plan is basically a state of being. It does not depend on anyone else. It is our attitude about our life that needs healing, initially from shallow and uncommitted to resolute and enthusiastic and not as a monthly or yearly routine but as a moment-by-moment investment. Recover your attention span. Sharpen your energy. Discipline your thoughts. This is your life purpose—mastering yourself—and then the big decisions can take care of themselves.

This is what mastery is all about. If you can conquer the forces around you in a meaningful way, bigger opportunities will literally arrive at your doorstep. Until they do, you know you are still "paving their way." Remember, it is not an intellectual game but requires real investment in your soul constitution, not illusion or delusion. There are no shortcuts.

Chapter Twelve: Energy Centres

Youth is not a time of life; it is a state of mind; it is not a matter of rosy cheeks, red lips and supple knees; it is a matter of the will, quality of the imagination, a vigour of the emotions; it is the freshness of the deep springs of life.
—Samuel Ullman

Our body is designed to support our spiritual energy identity. It is aligned for the work of spiritual entities, such as ourselves, who come from the universe. Adjustments in the process of our formation have been made to assist the subtleties of living on planet Earth, and we are an ongoing creation. Having an intellect is an example of such an alteration. Having a body does not change the dynamics of our energy identity. When we do not respect and honour our spiritual needs, we can create illness and disease by our thought processes (the energy we receive becomes limited, and therefore, there is less energy available for our body's demands). Because of these thoughts, we can divide our natures instead of living their unity and alignment. When we work against our spiritual nature, our physical body reflects it.

Without oneness of being, we are out-of-balance. When this happens, we can lose our big-picture perspective and become like a planet that is not aligned in its own galaxy system. This can be a very frightening idea when we are taking ourselves for granted and thinking we are somehow worthless or trashing our energy with reckless abandon. When we do this, we are being disloyal to our two natures and insincere in how we treat our body and soul.

We are a precious piece of the universe—perfect and functional like any of the stars or planets we see. You can devise in this vast galaxy we are presently a part of we are also a planet like planet Earth. Visualize what would happen if we did not have the sun. (We can call the sun our energy alignment.) Where would we be? The sun affects the life and death of a planet, but in between this life-and-death scenario, there are many specifics of causes and effects of our impact on it, particularly in relation to the way we as a race use the planet and its subsequent exposure to that impact, which we can liken to our life of ups and downs.

How do we use our body's energy centres, and what are our thought contributions to it? Are we one with it, being in tune with its earthly needs as the vehicle of our soul to run efficiently to provide for us the best ambiance? In other words, we need to live our constitution. After all, it was definitely set up for that.

We are not delving more deeply into any of this; it is to help us relate it to our own sophistication of our aura in receiving refined energy. It is indeed a subject that deserves more explanation, particularly in relation to the energy changes that have resulted in the refinement of how these centres receive energy. Our life and how we live it is governed by the spiritual energy that feeds it. We have refined from feeling beings with little organization and refinement to over-organized and refined beings with little feeling. You can assess for yourself if this is progression or repression. In the past, the process by which we absorbed energy was different than the way we do today. When we were only feeling beings, we operated with one perception and the energy came through that process. The other centres were there receiving energy in a limited capacity but inactive in the mainstream thought processes of our life.

Today we are four-perception beings evolving to a fifth perception. We are more complicated spiritually, so the energy feeding us is more sophisticated and the route of the energy has refined to meet our energy enlightenment demands. We can never have fixed ideas about this process because it will always be dependent on how we evolve and refine with those demands. It is the same as the word of God delivered through his prophets. It is delivered to our state of consciousness at the time, but the prophets who came after Moses had gradually added more and more truth to the word of God because we were ready and available to confront it. The perceptions we have today were not available then. Continuity is like a spiralling upward circle, the (imagined) end always heralding a new beginning.

Our life is affected by the energy centres consistent with the spiritual energy available to it. We have seven energy centres, and each of these centres relates to a specific growth pattern we have as a soul which is a prerequisite to it opening and operating efficiently. If we envisage our experiences rotating our energy in an upward spiral, we keep repeating a rotation of seven but always as we grow spiritually, at expanded levels of consciousness. Many realities are in the nature of six because the seventh is always a "God" space. It is the same with our energy centres, hence the number of the "devil" being portrayed as six (three of them for the lower states of consciousness)—because in the seventh level the devil has substituted God for himself. It is not necessary to know any of this at this level, because what we are not ready for we will experience only on an intellectual level and be unable to absorb. It can interfere with our progress as we may dwell on what we don't understand instead of flowing with what we do and allow our angels to train us in the solving of any mysteries when we are ready to engage them.

To facilitate our recognition, we can divide our energy centres up into seven diverse ideas about ourselves, each of which are in alignment or out of alignment with using the energy centres to our advantage or disadvantage.

Soul Acknowledgment

The first energy centre that receives energy supports our recognition of our true identity as a soul; our acknowledging of this soul identity helps to expand the energy available to our first chakra, and how much we live this truth determines the amount of energy that enters there. All the information we have been learning about awakening is all lived in this energy centre. As we awaken, we learn that we want energy, that we are energy, and how we think impacts on how we feel because our awareness of being a soul literally expands our energy centre receptor for an increase in energy. Similarly, if we ascend in our consciousness and then suddenly halt our transformation or become demoralized, we can descend, much like a plane losing altitude because of engine failure. We decrease our energy intake from a large pipe to a straw. In other words, we go from a finely tuned athlete to being on life support. Preferably we need to view these experiences as a test for us to elevate our consciousness yet again and a momentary glitch in our apparatus, thus keeping our energy momentum while we navigate a shift in attitude. Remember, you don't have to move out of home, give notice at your employment, or divorce your spouse. A change in attitude is merely shifting focus to the details of our thoughts and healing them or endeavouring to have little or no thoughts. It is best we patiently assess our present situation and how we can refine it, not make rash decisions to change our circumstances but rather heal the improprieties there.

The energy intake is what makes us happy in our life, fulfilled or unfulfilled. It makes or breaks our life opportunity. Our destiny is continually determined by the acceptance or rejection of our spiritual realities, whether we have an abundance of energy to back our life or a minimum to survive. We first address this learning in our first seven years. Up to the ages of two and three, we are still usually very aware of our soul identity.

Because we may have developed a liking to being catered to, we may conclude some truths we learn about are unfair. It is part of the stretching of our comfort zones to let truth in. We have to ask ourselves how cruel is it to live in a mouse hole when we are this magnificent, powerful, omnipotent spirit from the universe? If we are unlimited strength and resource, it is strange that we prefer to play dumb and desire to be catered to. It is difficult to reconcile or comprehend, but it is what many of us have learnt or been taught to do. The other unusual behaviour we have all developed is to hold onto someone else as if our whole life will plunge into the depths of despair without them and to defend our motives for doing this, as if our future was threatened. We can fly and be anywhere with anyone of our choosing whenever we want. There is never any reason to be anxious about others. Love unconditionally—this is the greatest gift of ourselves we can offer anyone.

I feel confident that part of our problem is when we hear the truth about who we are, we want to reject it, possibly even dismiss it, because we are afraid of our own power. We may want someone to save us, thus avoiding any risk taking on our part, but our potential is equal in energy to the prophets who offered their lives in the service of the truth. Embracing erudition, we may now choose to develop our inherent ability instead of wanting others to manifest to help us. Besides, once we apprehend the realization they are merely messengers and not the actual message, we can relax with our own inner truth, accepting the individuality of their message for us with gratitude, and develop it to heal any insecurity or anxiety we may have.

We come to planet Earth to change the status quo and to return to the purity of who we are. It is not easy to alter the course of our life, but if we have found incentive, it is inevitable. We need to trust our angels can provide the pathways back to our omnipotence. They can.

This war against our past tendencies to live who we really are is first waged in our first cycle. We come in (reincarnate) with our energy pure, and then we have our first stumbling block to overcome. If we heal this, we can more easily find our way to awakening. An explanation of this mysterious block follows.

Our First Blockage

In our first seven years, we pick up concepts that affect the way we view life, particularly after three years of age, although it can occur as early as six months. This is a fundamental part of the healing we are going to require on planet Earth. This concept engenders a type of fear around living our destiny, which is a misunderstanding. This concept then surfaces at varying crucial times in our life and can make us cower in the face of the fear we have around it. Usually, but not always, it is in a similar way to what we observed one of our parents or someone else influential in our early life do during our first seven years.

Because it is stimulated several times, eventually we have to overcome our timidity and heal it as part of our life mission. Although we can say it is a duplicated behaviour copied usually from a loved one, we did have free will at the time to adopt it or not. We may have a twin or other siblings who chose not to. The reason we do assume the blockage is because we usually have past life tendencies to heal around this misunderstanding, as has our parent who demonstrated the same fear. This parent is really only playing out his or her own script, which we wrote ourselves into. For many, if they can overcome this blockage in an otherwise unproductive spiritual life, it can be their spiritual purpose.

There is a blockage profile that addresses this and takes an hour that can be done by a spiritual consultant which I really recommend. In the absence of its availability, you can begin to investigate limitations one of the people in your early life had that you may have copied and developed into your own style. We can liken it to say a dread of drowning, which will automatically make you go through life avoiding water. One day it will become critical to address it because somehow it invites a confrontation for you where it is unavoidable. It might be a flood or a boating accident or someone you love experiencing difficulty. Or you may have someone teach your children to swim and this helps to heal it as you watch and learn the skills of swimming. Avoiding troublesome issues does not heal them. Facing them dilutes their power over us and in time, makes them subservient.

Usually it is not a blockage about drowning, but it is an easy example. It is really more likely to be a fear of rejection, not being good enough, being found out, not being perfect, being abandoned, dreading criticism, or any other concept like this. It is not immediately obvious to us, but as we are given the dates we lived it, we usually recall it painfully.

You may think it is normal to have those limitations, but it really is not. It does affect the way you live your life and how much negative energy you allow to affect you when you live the concern instead of the feeling of its solution. You can make decisions in your life based on your fears instead of your true direction. You may even marry people you have no real love for because of the disquiet. You may even divorce people you have real love for because they stimulate your anxiety and you don't want to deal with it. These are the types of influences such blockages can have on our whole life and the decisions we make.

It is good to remember, as I was myself taught, that every problem brings with it its own unique solution. Finding these solutions is how we accelerate our spiritual growth. When you heal the blockage, it is a profound introduction to freedom. You literally can feel invincible because you are amazed at the relief of releasing this limitation. It is definitely worth investing in soul-discovery and its eventual healing.

When we live this energy centre in-balance, we understand we are a soul and acknowledge it is necessary for us to be loyal to our journey on planet Earth and to discover our "soul identity" as distinct from the planetary identity we have assumed for a short time.

Welcome to planet Earth. I sincerely hope your stay here is happy, joyful, and productive. Now you know who you are you can change what doesn't fit the life of an energy being such as yourself. The power is in your hands always.

Note: The other six energy centres will be covered at another time to avoid introducing an excess of intellectualizing on spiritual realities we don't have a frame for presently.

Chapter Thirteen: Cycles of Life

Years may wrinkle the skin, but to give up enthusiasm wrinkles the soul. Worry, fear, self distrust bows the heart and turns the spirit back to dust.

—*Samuel Ullman*

Let us recap what we have learnt about our soul's constitution.

We are a soul, which has a body to navigate its way through certain experiences on planet Earth. This planet offers us the opportunity to discover what creases or rather inhibitions and/or limitations we may have the tendency to allow to remain in our energy. A process of self-reflection best executes this discovery.

First our parents offer us a mirror of our past (before we were born). Whatever misunderstandings one of them has encountered in this lifetime, we must have in some way likewise have lived before them, and these misinterpretations of our truth created the inhibitions or limitations we were or still are confronted with today.

By having our mother and father to observe, we are already way ahead of the game of life because when we work out their trouble, we can fix ours and be well on our way to enlightenment. This is the big first challenge to overcome.

Our first seven years help us absorb their concepts and their truth, and we spend the rest of our lives working on these impediments as we go through each of our cycles. Each seven years we get a new book to read about ourselves through changing our cycles.

Zero to Seven: Identifying

The first seven years are all about the past and our parents. We could each of us write a book on this cycle of our own journey. There are many concepts we observed, picked up, copied, enacted, and extended that helped form the personality we have now. We chose these parents as much for their confusion as for the refinement they offered us. Because our first mission has always been to heal the past (past lives that is), they are the key to revealing that. They usually help us identify ourselves through one parent mirroring our limitations and the other inspiring us to reach our potential. Either way, we need to break new ground beyond their achievements.

Seven to Fourteen: Purposeful

The second seven-year cycle is all about learning how the planet we are on functions and how we operate within its terms of reference and gathering facts, available for when we are ready to mature; we learn how to obtain our prerequisites to achieve what we came to do. It is learning about our mission, the possibilities it may embody, and where the societal change we have passion to pursue may fit (if we have the cycles in balance) as we develop our intellect. It is the age of reason. Traditionally there are many whys we ask at this stage of our development. The answers to these questions are pivotal to us, as we are open to learning. We examine ideas about our future. We may want to join the fire brigade or drive equipment or fly planes or follow in the career path of our father and/or mother. This is all experimental. They may be symbolic careers of strength, endurance, and helping others, which may all be echoes of the feeling of our path and purpose. As time rolls on, we can define it better, and we commence to recognize the vision of what it is we came to do beyond healing our concepts.

Fourteen to Twenty-One: Fortifying

The third cycle is all about breaking out of the past mode of behaviour to fortify our true identity. We enlist a little physical help here to strengthen our resolve. Our body has certain hormones, which affect us, and in addition to growing into physical maturity, our minds want to break away from the traditions of the past. For a time we are energized by our desire to meet spiritual challenges consistent with the physical maturity our body is undergoing. It is all a little confusing because we are accelerating our refinement, and if we want to hold onto comfort zones, we will feel very challenged. We will feel angry and aggressive about situations because we don't know how to handle these confrontations. But it makes us process life spontaneously, and this usually helps us to grow spiritually. We may rebel against our parents because we feel as if they are limiting us by treating us as immature or unreliable. Life can feel like a battle against restrictions. If we have learnt self-discipline, we will not have difficulty meeting the new challenges. If we have not, we may follow the crowd rather than following the force stirring inside us.

Twenty-One to Twenty-Eight: Resurgence

Our fourth cycle is all about regrouping the past three, cleaning up whatever there is to heal, and reclaiming our spiritual identity. We start to take on some more maturity, evaluate what our first seven years were about, and learn how to navigate our spiritual ship toward our destiny, thus enabling us to feel good about our life. We can regroup our second cycle of purpose and what that represented, as well as quelling the rebellion we may have felt in our third cycle, evaluating it with real building blocks and an awareness of where we need to navigate through the waters of life right now. If our first cycle was very toxic, we may feel suicidal at this time in our life or we may behave recklessly, inviting the potential of fate to shorten our life expectancy. Once we make it to twenty-five, we are usually more or less over the hump and can mature steadily. Ambition can make its presence felt as we demand to be recognized as mature adults, and spiritually, if we have developed true to our cycles, we are definitely ready for larger opportunities.

Twenty-Eight to Thirty-Five: Verify

In our fifth cycle, we are searching for more revelations again about our spiritual opportunity on planet earth. What does it mean? Who are we, and where did we come from to arrive where we are right now? We may want to study more metaphysical truths than we ever did in our life up till now. It is like the sea of emotion has become subdued and we can understand more clearly the path we are taking. We seek to verify with more definition and maturity what it is we have come to achieve spiritually.

Thirty-Five to Forty-Two: Foresight

Our sixth cycle is gathering abundance. We may mistake it for material abundance, but we are directing our passion toward a specific goal, target, or ambition we now know we want to take without the many obstructions we may have felt in our life up till now. We are more concerned about timing and what we desire to do to feel fulfilled. We can reach the pinnacle of success in a career or life opportunities we have invested in. Whatever it is, we feel driven by it and are looking toward its success. We look forward with vision.

Forty-Two to Forty-Nine: Acuity

Our seventh cycle is where we reap the rewards of what we have invested in ourselves spiritually. If we have not participated in acquiring spiritual truths, we may feel unfulfilled and commence searching for the why of our life. We may feel driven to find what we are passionate to do, as if time is running out. We may blame our relationships or act out of character; we can lose our fortune and have to start again. It is all about our spiritual rewards for a life lived in our purpose. When we don't feel it, we can become anxious without really knowing why.

Forty-Nine to Fifty-Six: Charisma

Our eighth cycle is where we again look at our lifetime and evaluate what it is we are doing here. We expand into a more charismatic person if we are true to our spiritual adventure and its timing. If not, we take an inventory of the positives and negatives of our time invested. It may happen on a subconscious level if we are really caught in illusions or delusions. We may feel it as being unsettled and nothing quite working for us as we think it should. We may have invested in a family maze instead of investing in ourselves and feel like our cup is empty because we did not get what we expected from our investments. This is where we make a decision whether we stay or go on planet Earth. If we are not accomplishing our soul's purpose, we often pass on during the next cycle.

The remaining cycles and more details on the cycles we will investigate in the future. We will not assimilate more that than this at this time.

Chapter Fourteen: Questions and Answers

Let us review the questions we asked in chapter one and assess the answers we have already uncovered in the book.

o **Why does life have ups and downs?**
   How we think—our thoughts—makes us emotional, which is where our ups and downs come from. If we expect, assume, and demand, we have nothing but disappointments, frustrations, and anger. We have to change that to a feeling perspective, which is all about gratitude for the opportunities we have in

life and making changes to what we innately know demands a paradigm shift. Investing in truth sows the seeds of inner serenity. The wisdom tree it sprouts will ascend to whatever height you as a soul permit it to. When you have answers from your soul's constitution, you can discover the journey rather than being dragged by fate.

The fates lead him who will—him who won't they drag.
—Seneca

o **Who is pulling the strings or making things happen, so to speak?**
We are. Our soul part is totally responsible for our life's encounters. How we think and act upon it determines how our life works. We, our feelings, our soul part, actually dictate how our life unfolds. If we are listening to our inner truth and following it, life is wonderful and abundant, building upon success after success. If we don't, we have learning lessons that our feelings, using their magnetic energy, pull us toward because we are wasting our lifetime. Hence, change has to happen to realign us.

Remember that what pulls the strings is the force hidden within; there lies the power to persuade, there the life—there, if one must speak out, the real man.
—Marcus Aurellius

o **Why do things happen to me?**
This answer is for the same reason as stated above. If we are living our intellectual ideas and ideals of life (programming), we allow incidences to manifest that we would prefer not to endure, but because we have chosen a low state of consciousness to learn through, this is our fate, which we can compare to hitting our head against a brick wall. What we can call hell is right here on planet Earth to live if we choose it, or through living illusion instead of our souls constitution. After a while we realize it hurts and we stop doing it. These are called learning curves. If we work with what feels right to do rather

than forcing the misconception of duty upon us, we can avoid difficulties in life. First, though, we need to truly discern what our inner truth is communicating.

There is something in every one of you that waits and listens for the sound of the genuine in yourself. It is the only true guide you will ever have. And if you cannot hear it, you will all of your life spend your days on the ends of strings that somebody else pulls.

—Howard Thurman
(American theologian, clergyman, and activist)

o **Why don't things happen for me?**
Whatever happens to us or does not happen for us are situations we have already chosen as our path and purpose. If we are envious of others' abundance, it is because we are not living in the middle of our own stream. We are instead standing on the embankment, being a spectator of our own life and distracted from its pursuit by others. In these circumstances, we live life's misadventures. The constitution of our soul, our inner truth, is the administrator of our life, and the sooner we communicate, coordinate, and recheck with it, the earlier we will become masterful in our consequential fate.

Envy is a symptom of lack of appreciation of our own uniqueness and self worth. Each of us has something to give that no one else has.

—Anonymous

A person often meets his destiny on the road he took to avoid it.

—Jean de La Fontaine

o **Where does luck come from?**
Each of us makes our own luck in life. If we follow our innate desires and hunches, we have a wonderful, fulfilling, and bountiful life. Sometimes our bounty may not be in a physical form because it is not part of our mission here. When we

align with our feelings, miracles can happen. Energy, when it builds, breaks previous known boundaries of awareness, and we therefore feel it as a miracle. We can compare it to that impossible to find a parking space scenario in the busiest of cities at peak traffic time. If we ask our angels and where we are going is part of our purpose, we trust and take the risk, and there is the parking space waiting for us. We can compare this happening to all challenges we believe are impossible for us to achieve. If it is part of our life plan, they show us miracles every day. Universal energy is boundless, limitless, all knowing, powerful, resourceful, and miracle making. When we are on the energy stream, others, even strangers, are of service to us. They make life's challenges appear trivial because our angels provide energy to unblock the entanglements. All people love energy—you showed up with all this energy—that makes them happy to have you around accordingly they treat you with respect and courtesy. When you leave the energy leaves with you and life becomes dull again for them.

Luck is what happens when preparation meets opportunity.

—Seneca

o **Where does fate come from?**
We are electromagnetic energy. We keep moving toward the people we most need to interact with. This is the force of our soul directing our fate. Regardless of what we think, we are still inaugurating our own experiences, which are either richly rewarding, frighteningly disturbing, or somewhere in between because they are necessary for us to develop as a soul. We can fortuitously meet the people who stimulate this healing or growth or both without realizing it is part of our design. If it is our idea to discover ourselves, we are enthusiastic and profoundly grateful for the life challenges we attract, or if not, we are trying to claw onto comfort zones and not heeding the need to alter our course. We then entice a more inopportune fate. We may have accidents, shocks, or things of this nature as a wakeup call.

There is no chance, no destiny, no fate, that can circumvent or hinder or control the firm resolve of a determined soul.

—Ella Wheeler Wilcox

o **Why do we have a life?**
A lifetime is a precious page of our destiny to us. In the universe, we do not have the opportunity to amend our energy fortunes like we do on planet Earth. Time is slowed down here, giving us the ability to subjugate our concepts and their inhibitions. The universe is more structured and defined, and it does not present us with the same opportunities to change our status quo. It can be this desire to refine that makes us choose a lifetime. This idea of redefining our energy has nothing to do with planetary notions. It is learning about our energy and how to make it less encumbered by concepts, illusions, and delusions.

Destiny itself is like a wonderful wide tapestry in which every thread is guided by an unspeakably tender hand, placed beside another thread and held and carried by a hundred others.

—Raincr Maria Rilke

o **Why do we get old?**
We are here only fleetingly. The whole planet is reflective for us while we live our brief sojourn. Whatever is happening to us is demonstrated in our surroundings. We can't help but become enlightened if we know this, because the opportunity for expansion is all around us. The aging process helps us identify with the time we arrive and the time we are leaving; we therefore must accept that planet Earth is not a home for us because we have no continuity here that we have control over. The closer we come to our time for departing, the more serious we become in our intentions to evaluate our accomplishments of understanding our soul constitution and

actioning its agenda. It also helps us identify with using our time productively, since it is limited.

The most violent revolutions in an individual's beliefs leave most of his old order standing. Time and space, cause and effect, nature and history, and one's own biography remain untouched. New truth is always a go between, a smoother over of transitions. It marries old opinions to new fact so as ever to show a minimum of jolt, a maximum of continuity.

—William James

o **Why do most people want to get married?**
When we come to planet Earth, we come with a list of grievances with others to heal. The first part of the healing process comes from within the family we incarnate into, where we become engrossed in an experimental laboratory to unearth our soul history through the symbolic nature of our emotions. We are auspiciously tied by fate together with an invisible cord to those around us. There are many levels of healing our parents can offer us. As we mature we are usually attracted to following the cultural tradition of our parents and others influential in our life, which may place emphasis on a search for a suitable person to share our life with. Often our traditions may overwhelm the constitution of our soul, our inner truth, in the choices we make, which may be why there are so many divorces. We may marry because of pressure from outside influences. If we marry and have a wonderful relationship and it ends in divorce, it may just signal the healing with our partner, or parent we had difficulty with is complete. We need to congratulate all those involved and foster new meaningful supportive friendships in its wake. A new member or members to our spiritual family we can add with this attitude. Usually if we do marry, like our parents before us, we desire to open a door to offer the same opportunity to other souls, who become our children. If we have clarified spiritually to a cultivated extent, the souls we invite to be our children will be even more refined than we are, and we can then in time learn from

them, if we open ourselves to that. It is like the quotes about continuity. This is continuity.

In youth we learn; in age we understand.
—Marie von Ebner-Eschenbach

o **Why don't some people get married?**
Some people who come to planet Earth do not come to heal relationships in this way. They may have bigger opportunities ahead of them and relationships may present as incompatible to their chosen path. The direction they have chosen is unique, as each person's is. They may have had many mazes around relationships and have chosen avoidance this lifetime. We cannot judge another's pathway, and we can only understand it in relation to our own unique consciousness. The children we have are not our children but souls travelling with us for a short time that provide endless enlightenment for our own journey. It is dangerous to judge others because all of us are still learning copious amounts about ourselves. Therefore, until we are at a very refined level, it is difficult for us to adequately even evaluate others. It is enough to use our interpretations of their actions as a reflection of our own self-learning, regardless of whether we view them as negative or positive. We need to be cautious about offering advice to people in this respect, particularly our children who possibly and hopefully are more enlightened presently or potentially than we are.

Marriage is like a cage; one sees the birds outside desperate to get in, and those inside equally desperate to get out.
—Michel de Montaigne

o **Why are we all different?**
A soul is a fully self-contained, powerful, unique vibration. We are not white, black, red, yellow, or chocolate. We are energy that is intelligent. We don't belong to a race, religion, creed, or gender; we have our own innate soul constitution from eons of time that is self-sufficient. We evolve in our own unique way under our own guidance and direction. We are too powerful

and self-sufficient to necessitate being saved. We solely require facts to deliver us to whatever we discern is our destination. We alone choose its passageways under the guidance of our angels.

We have generally had numerous lifetimes in various continents for diverse reasons, such as the state of consciousness of a continent/country that may have helped us to heal a tendency we are having difficulty with. We may choose a specific race of people for that. Some races have more feeling energy naturally. Some tend to be more in survival, a natural way to learn about ourselves. There are such unique reasons for each of us to incarnate in the country and even the distinct locality we are born. It may take us years of discerning to properly understand why.

In the past, we may have been a slave trader one lifetime and the next lifetime returned as a slave, and maybe in this new lifetime as a slave, our master was one of the slaves we sold. This is the extraordinary circumstance of the truth of our soul constitution. If we have a strong racial discrimination, we essentially need to return as a person of the race we have discriminated strongly against because our love energy has been violated with malevolence, and this has to be healed.

In every concrete individual, there is a uniqueness that defies formulation. We can feel the touch of it and recognize its taste so to speak, relishing or disliking, as the case may be, but we can give no ultimate account of it, and we have in the end simply to admire the creator.

—William James

o **Is there really a God?**
The facts are that we are a reflection of God. It can be whatever the prophets have described. If we look at whoever has inspired us the most in our life by their deeds, we can see that reflection within them. We can likewise mirror it within ourselves when we are happy with whom we are. We don't necessarily have to believe in God as a rigid belief initially because it comes at a certain level of enlightenment naturally. If it is forced, it may

be prone to many disappointments and distrust. We first have to believe in our omnipotence and trust the serendipitous life we can have through working with our angels. Appreciate that is all we require to reach wherever our mission leads us to. If the subject of God interferes with our own self-development, it is best left on a mental shelf until the time comes for us to evolve into the big-picture recognition of it. If we have some very fixed pictures about it, we may have been infected with dogma in our early life, and it is best to trust the truth we feel inside rather than the one we have been taught. It will ultimately lead us home. Our constitution can educate us to understand our life spontaneously. Sometimes as we advance spiritually, we may wish to reverse our beliefs. This is merely the natural process of opening ourselves to more truth as we become ready for it, which may have been shrouded in mystery or illusion before. Patience with all our present and erstwhile feelings is a very commendable attribute. Rather than debating what one doesn't know, it is preferable to let our understandings develop fortuitously and in the interim hang out a sign on our beliefs "gone fishing."

When I admire the beauty of a sunset or the beauty of the moon, my soul expands in worship of the Creator.

—Mahatma Gandhi

o **If there is a God, what is he doing all day?**
The planet we are on has a state of consciousness, as we do. This reflects the general consciousness of the populace of planet Earth. Each city has a state of consciousness, as does each town and each country and each person. We choose where we are born because of its state of consciousness. The planet may not be perfect, but neither are the people who dwell here. All of us can benefit by learning from our life encounters or we would not be here. Instead of looking around for others' solutions, we are obliged to find them ourselves by taking responsibility for our own life. If life were perfect, what would we learn? When we become too enlightened for a place, we move. It is the best direction we can take. If we are blaming a place for

our difficulties in life, then it may be necessary for us to find somewhere more clarified to live. If God were to interfere in our process, it could be too powerful for us to absorb. Because the planet is reflective, we may have heightened experiences of our learning, such as storms creating tsunamis, fires turning to infernos, hurricanes that are beyond recorded history, and earthquakes that destroy landmasses. We may lose our comfort zones overnight, and perhaps this we can call God expressing his love for us. Putting us in survival—our feelings—means we can live our potential more rapidly. I feel confident God does not intervene because he trusts that we will find our way eventually, but we may require a little prodding at times when we become very fixed in our ways. He has certainly exhausted every opportunity available to back us to refine.

Again I bid you to speak not so freely of God, who is your All, but speak rather and understand one another, neighbour unto neighbour, a god unto a god.

—Kahlil Gibran

o **Why isn't God fixing things?**
Each situation is perfect for the learning that is essential to the success of our life purpose. If it were not, we would fix it ourselves. We are self-sufficient; usually we don't desire the help we seek. We rather need guidance. Using children as an example, if we take away their experiments in self-education, how will they learn? If we have refinement available and waiting for us, how will we develop creativity? If misguided thoughts, which we have, are conquered by others, how will we learn to overcome them ourselves? If life was completely defined, why bother coming to planet Earth?

We have, I am sure, heard of God being all merciful, all forgiving, all discerning, all compassionate, etc. This is similarly true for who we are when we are living our purity. Why are we here? For the very reason we want him to fix our life difficulties. Your energy is more than enough to do the job it came to do. That is why there are angels—they are delegated the tasks their wisdom is suited for. You will benefit from listening in to yourself and what you complain about. There is a key to your purpose. The more we refine ourselves, the more it is our opportunity to help others to refine.

We don't do it only because we are compassionate but mainly we desire to do it for our own development. Without outflow, we stagnate. This is why planet Earth is such a wonderful place to come to—it has endless opportunity at every level of our self-advancement. We are never without challenges. Remember whatever we want others to do, always becomes our own opportunity.

Isn't it time you found your *footprints in the sands of time* on this planet?

> Verily your deeds will be brought back to you, as if you yourself were the creator of your own punishment.
> —Muhammad

o **Why do I want to know about my soul identity? How will it help me?**
If there is one thing that I hope you take with you from this book, it is the desire to learn about yourself. Everything has been written to prompt you to do that! Why? Because you are your soul, and it is your constitution. You are not your body. What happens in your soul happens there first and then filters down to your body. As your intellect is part of your body, we can say your personality is directly affected by your soul discoveries or spiritual obliviousness. Whether you are a people person or a person who likes to avoid people will all be determined by the clarity or blockages you have in your soul. You are here on planet Earth for that. Would this book be the word of Spirit if it did not tell you that your inner truth is the most important discovery you can make and instead told you that your life here is wonderful and why change it?

The beauty of who you are is knocking at your door, demanding to be let in. Open the door; there is nothing to fear there. It is you who are knocking at your own door. Let you into your life; you will discover the pathways to the most profound and nurturing love with the evolvement of your truth. You will walk tall, feel confident, have compassion, live fulfilment, be contented, be magnanimous, be omnipotent, and understand your immortality. Is there really any other choice? Personally, I don't think so. Sure, the pathway to owning all that you are is rocky, but what else is there to do? Whatever makes it difficult, remember, you are the one who placed those impediments there, and only you can take them away. Forgive you! What is there to lose? Concede the truth that there is a place next to God for you, and he is waiting for you to obliterate the inhibitions on your pathway opening possibilities for him to enjoy your fellowship and wisdom again. How do you respond to that? Are you too busy in your life of illusions to answer his call? Would he say to his angels, "Remove those hindrances so he/she can be with me again"? No, he would not because you would return a weakened being through being unable to navigate your maze. He respects you to find your own way. He knows who you are and what you can do. It is you who needs to be reminded of who you really are.

There is an affirmation here that may help you with this: "I trust my part in the purity of God. I am his reflection, as I am for all those who seek his will."

It is the unseen and the spiritual in people that determines the outward and the actual.

—Thomas Carlyle

The Spiritual Internet

The Internet we use every day is a very good reflection of what we call Spirit. It is a bigger picture of information than most of us are really ready for as we awaken to our awareness of being a soul and reverse our habit of living our life upside down and inside out. One possibility to help us do this is to realize in our everyday living we are not a role but a soul.

When we play a role, we are limiting ourselves to a small picture, which can be compared to that of a computer without access to the Internet. When we have our Internet connection, we have unlimited resources to all manner of information. When we are connected with our angels and we have a working relationship with them, we can enquire of all mysteries that cloud our life and discernment. This is like the Internet.

In the beginning of us exploring our communication with them, we can often work with a yes and no answer technique, particularly if we have had a profile with a spiritual consultant. After a while, through practice, we learn to accept their communications coming directly to us, which come in downloads, much like we download information from the Internet.

As we work with this over the years, we learn how to trigger responses from our own memory bank. We can ask our feelings these questions; our guidance backs all of our endeavours to find the information necessary for our search of soul-discovery.

Our guidance has a much greater influence on training us than perhaps we could ever realize. I learn more about this every day. They light up objects for us with energy, expanding the goal posts of our life's field of vision each and every day. This then makes us have inspired thoughts about it. We may turn the car radio on and hear a song, and the words may make us feel like crying. Then we may go somewhere else and the song will be playing again and we can't help but wonder at the coincidence. Then when we hear it a third time, we are ready to accept it is our angels communicating to us. It is a very successful system of interfacing with our wisdom and our angels. There are many other ways they broadcast messages to us, such as through billboards, sign posts, lettered registration plates, or other ways that we may happen to notice. At times they will even communicate with us through the news we watch if we have inspired impressions or warnings. We may feel energy around a story or event and feel a surge of curiosity well within us.

Conclusion

This is the constitution of the soul, our inner truth. It is all the questions answered you may have as you begin your search.

The information in *The Constitution of Our Soul* with help and guidance can be a powerful, packed opportunity that may, depending on how you invest in its tools and techniques and your exposure to the content of your constitution, be a good five to seven years worth of unfolding if you are beginning at the awakening level and without spiritual courses to accelerate your growth. Of course, we have to invest in ourselves to reap the rewards of making our feelings our first priority in our life. Ultimately it will all depend on how we shape our life to meet any changes in our attitude to ourselves.

If you would like to learn more about any of the services mentioned, I am going to direct you to a website (see back cover for address) that will help you with your search. There is a book two, but it will wait until there is a demand for more information.

To finish the book, I would like to first express my gratitude to each of you, the readers, for allowing me the opportunity to share with you the message and my experiences of living it. I hope it offers you the sound of your soul's music. Many thousands of years ago, I came to deliver that message and instead found my pride and ego more attractive. Although time has moved on and many more concepts have been added through neglect of the solution of this simple message, it is as relevant today as it was then.

I would also like to thank all of those people I have been able to share with prior to writing the book. In the process of training them in the tools and techniques I myself was taught, they gave me the opportunity to consolidate and define the wisdom I have to share. This in turn has helped to refine the message and assist even more people to open the door to living their true potential.

Of course, none of it was possible without the total commitment of my angels, who were there every step of the way. Many times they carried me when I lost the will to live my purpose, felt overwhelmed by the burden of it, and/or rebelled against it, and without them, of course, there would be nothing to share.

Yours in Spirit,

Kristy Kaye